25 IMMUTABLE LAWS OF GEOPOLITICAL STRATEGIES

BY
TODD PRICE & AMBER OQUINDO

25 IMMUTABLE LAWS OF GEOPOLITICAL STRATEGIES

Published by: USA Publishing Hub
Printed In United States of America
GCTI-LLC | Central Point, OR. 97502
www.usapublishinghub.com

"Geopolitics is the art of understanding the world's equilibrium points, where the balance of power, perception, and principle determines a nation's legacy."

- Todd M Price

INTRODUCTION

In a world defined by shifting alliances, emergent technologies, and ever-present challenges, the art and science of geopolitical strategy demand a framework that transcends fleeting trends. **The 25 Immutable Laws of Geopolitical Strategy** provide a framework, drawing from history, theory, and practice to illuminate timeless principles that guide nations, leaders, and organizations toward stability, influence, and resilience.

Crafted with a blend of rigorous academic research and practical insights, these laws serve as cornerstones for understanding the complexities of global politics. From the visionary leadership of Churchill to the delicate balancing acts in multilateral diplomacy, the laws encapsulate lessons from the past while providing actionable guidance for navigating the future. Each law is not merely theoretical but grounded in case studies, research, and actionable insights, making them accessible and applicable across contexts.

At its core, this collection seeks to equip policymakers, scholars, and students with the tools to decode geopolitical phenomena, predict shifts, and shape outcomes. By examining leadership, alliances, economic strategies, and more, **The 25 Immutable Laws** offers a comprehensive lens to view the dynamics of power, conflict, and cooperation.

Whether used as a guide for strategic decision-making or a foundation for academic exploration, these laws are essential for anyone seeking to understand and influence the global stage.

AUTHORS' BIOGRAPHY

Todd M. Price, MBA, Ph.D.(c)

Todd M. Price is a distinguished expert in counter-terrorism and international security, with over two decades of service in the U.S. Army. A co-founder of the Global Counter-Terrorism Institute (GCTI) and President of the Global CT Institute Foundation, Price has spearheaded innovative solutions in combating terrorism through operational and academic approaches.

Currently serving as Chair of the Master's in International Security Studies at the Paris Graduate School - Innovative Knowledge Institute, Price combines his vast field experience with a dedication to cultivating the next generation of global security leaders. He has received numerous awards, including a humanitarian service award and recognition for peacekeeping operations in the Middle East and North Africa.

Price's philosophy emphasizes the power of soft diplomacy and education in fostering international cooperation and preempting the roots of terrorism. His pioneering work with the Price-Oquindo DTM™ predictive risk model showcases his commitment to leveraging artificial intelligence and data-driven strategies to create actionable solutions for global security challenges.

Amber R. Oquindo, MSHS, Ph.D.(c)

Amber R. Oquindo is a thought leader in counter-terrorism education and advocates for using knowledge for global change. She holds a Master of Science in Homeland Security Management and a Bachelor of Arts in Political Science, with prestigious certifications from FEMA. Oquindo's expertise lies in terrorism recruitment mechanisms, radicalization, and propaganda dissemination.

As the Curriculum Development Director for GCTI, she designs educational programs that address the complex dimensions of terrorism and security. Her collaborative work with NGOs in marginalized regions like the Middle East highlights her commitment to grassroots empowerment and countering extremism through education.

Amber Oquindo believes in the transformative power of learning to address critical societal challenges, advocating for programs that blend intellectual rigor with practical solutions. Her leadership in developing the Price-Oquindo DTM™ model has cemented her role as a pioneer in predictive modeling for terrorism risk assessment.

THE 25 IMMUTABLE LAWS OF GEOPOLITICAL STRATEGY

1. The Law of Leadership
2. The Law of the Battlefield
3. The Law of Perception
4. The Law of Focus
5. The Law of Exclusivity
6. The Law of Duality
7. The Law of the Opposite
8. The Law of Division
9. The Law of Perspective
10. The Law of Line Extension
11. The Law of Sacrifice
12. The Law of Adaptability
13. The Law of Alliances
14. The Law of Sovereignty
15. The Law of Balance
16. The Law of Asymmetry
17. The Law of Strategic Depth
18. The Law of Encirclement
19. The Law of Deterrence
20. The Law of Proximity
21. The Law of Relevance
22. The Law of Resilience
23. The Law of Innovation
24. The Law of Continuity
25. The Law of Strategic Patience

TABLE OF CONTENTS

1. THE LAW OF LEADERSHIP

SECTION 1: THE LAW OF LEADERSHIP

Abstract

Leadership forms the foundation of geopolitical strategy, influencing how nations navigate challenges and seize opportunities. *The Law of Leadership* identifies key traits influencing global outcomes and providing actionable lessons. Historical case studies and peer-reviewed research offer examples and support practical applications. Understanding these principles enhances decision-making and leadership effectiveness in complex geopolitical contexts.

Introduction

Leadership in geopolitics goes beyond authority. It shapes national vision, guides strategy, and builds resilience during uncertainty. Effective leaders influence a nation's trajectory. Their actions affect domestic stability and international relations. Key qualities of impactful leadership are explored through historical and modern examples. These examples emphasize their critical role in shaping outcomes.

Key Components of The Law of Leadership

1. Visionary Thinking

A leader's vision sets the strategic direction for their nation. Winston Churchill exemplified visionary leadership during World War II. His ability to articulate a compelling vision rallied the British people and secured critical alliances, influencing the war's outcome.

- **Case Study**: Churchill's speeches and policies demonstrated how vision can galvanize a nation. His leadership has been extensively analyzed, including in John Lukacs' *Five Days in London: May 1940* (New Haven: Yale University Press, 1999).

2. Decisive Action

Effective leaders act quickly and with purpose. Informed, timely decisions distinguish success from failure. For instance, Franklin D. Roosevelt implemented the New Deal policies that stabilized the U.S. economy and restored public confidence.

- **Example:** Roosevelt's actions addressed economic challenges and reshaped public trust. For more information, see Gavin Wright's "The New Deal and the Modern Economy," *Oxford Review of Economic Policy* 26, no.3 (2010): 386–404, https://doi.org/10.1093/oxrep/grq020.

3. Emotional Intelligence

Understanding and addressing people's needs and emotions is critical for building trust and inspiring unity. High emotional intelligence strengthens leadership, particularly during crises.

- **Research Insight:** A study by Ashkanasy and Humphrey in *Leadership Quarterly* highlights how emotional intelligence enabled leaders to manage COVID-19-related crises effectively (Ashkanasy and Humphrey, "Current Trends in Emotion and Leadership," *Leadership Quarterly* 32, no.5 [2021]: 101404, https://doi.org/10.1016/j.leaqua.2021.101404).

Application of The Law

1. Military Leadership

Successful military leaders adapt strategies to evolving conditions.

General Dwight D. Eisenhower's orchestration of the D-Day invasion showcased his strategic brilliance and ability to unify disparate allied forces.

2. Diplomatic Leadership

Pragmatic diplomacy strengthens international stability and cooperation.

Angela Merkel's leadership as Germany's Chancellor reinforced the European Union during economic and political crises. Her approach emphasized negotiation and resilience.

3. Economic Leadership

Visionary economic policies drive transformative development. Lee Kuan Yew' implemented strategies that turned Singapore into a global economic hub. His leadership is thoroughly analyzed in Lee Kuan Yew's From Third World to First: The Singapore Story (New York: HarperCollins, 2000).

Lessons Learned

1. Leadership is contextual, but universal qualities—vision, decisiveness, and emotional intelligence—transcend situations.
2. Geopolitical instability often correlates with ineffective leadership, as demonstrated during the collapse of the Soviet Union.
3. Leadership must evolve in response to new challenges, balancing tradition with innovation.

Conclusion

The Law of Leadership demonstrates that nations rise or fall based on the strength of their leadership. Leaders who exhibit vision, decisiveness, and emotional intelligence set their countries on paths to success. Further exploration of *The 25 Immutable Laws of Geopolitical Strategy* provides tools for understanding and applying these principles in today's complex geopolitical landscape.

References

- Lukacs, John. *Five Days in London: May 1940.* New Haven: Yale University Press, 1999.
- Wright, Gavin. "The New Deal and the Modern Economy." *Oxford Review of Economic Policy* 26, no. 3 (2010): 386–404. https://doi.org/10.1093/oxrep/grq020.
- Ashkanasy, Neal M., and Ronald H. Humphrey. "Current Trends in Emotion and Leadership." *Leadership Quarterly* 32, no. 5 (2021): 101404. https://doi.org/10.1016/j.leaqua.2021.101404.
- Lee, Kuan Yew. *From Third World to First: The Singapore Story.* New York: HarperCollins, 2000.

SECTION 2: THE LAW OF THE BATTLEFIELD

Abstract

Whether physical, ideological, or virtual, the battlefield remains a critical domain in geopolitical strategy. *The Law of the Battlefield* emphasizes the need to understand and adapt to the complexities of conflict environments to achieve strategic objectives. Historical and modern examples illustrate the application of battlefield dynamics. Peer-reviewed research and case studies provide insights into how nations navigate these complex domains effectively.

Introduction

The battlefield is more than a physical space—it is an arena where strategy, technology, and human ingenuity converge. Whether in traditional military conflicts or ideological and cyber confrontations, success is determined by the ability to analyze, anticipate, and dominate the battlefield's unique characteristics.

Key Components of The Law of the Battlefield

1. Understanding Terrain

Knowing the physical or ideological terrain of the battlefield is vital for success. From mountainous Afghanistan regions to Mosul's urban warfare, effective strategy begins with understanding the environment.

- **Case Study:** The Soviet-Afghan War (1979–1989) demonstrates how terrain influenced outcomes. The Afghan mujahideen's familiarity with the mountainous terrain outmatched Soviet forces, highlighting the importance of local knowledge (Glenn E. Curtis, *Afghanistan: A Country Study* [Washington, DC: Library of Congress, 2008], https://www.loc.gov/item/2010292299/).

2. Anticipating Enemy Movements

Success on the battlefield often hinges on predicting and countering the enemy's actions. This requires intelligence, reconnaissance, and adaptability.

- **Example:** The Allied forces' success in World War II's Operation Overlord (D-Day) was due in part to superior intelligence and deception tactics, including the use of Operation Bodyguard to mislead German forces (Michael D. Doubler, *Closing with the Enemy: How GIs Fought the War in Europe, 1944–1945* [Lawrence: University Press of Kansas, 1994], https://www.kansaspress.ku.edu/9780700612497.html).

3. Leveraging Technology

Technology often shifts the balance of power on the battlefield. From radar in World War II to drones and cyberweapons today, innovation is key.

- **Research Insight:** The role of drones in modern warfare demonstrates this principle. For example, their use in counterinsurgency operations in Pakistan provided real-time intelligence and precision strikes (Peter W. Singer, "The Predator Comes Home," *Foreign Affairs* 93, no. 3 [2014]: 122–38, https://www.foreignaffairs.com/articles/united-states/2014-05-01/predator-comes-home).

Application of The Law

1. Conventional Warfare

Traditional battlefields demand mastery of logistics, coordination, and firepower. The U.S. military's Desert Storm operation exemplifies this, showcasing how air superiority and ground coordination can overwhelm an enemy.

2. Ideological Battlegrounds

Non-physical battlefields, such as those in the War on Terror, require strategies to counter extremist ideologies. This includes undermining propaganda and fostering counter-narratives through education and diplomacy.

3. Cyber Battlefields

The rise of cyber warfare has created a new domain of conflict. Nations now fight for dominance in cyberspace, where battles are waged over information, infrastructure, and influence.

- **Case Study:** Russia's 2007 cyberattack on Estonia crippled the nation's infrastructure, underscoring the vulnerability of digital systems (Joshua Davis, "The Secret War," Wired, August 21, 2007, https://www.wired.com/2007/08/ff-estonia/).

Lessons Learned

1. A comprehensive understanding of the battlefield is essential for effective physical, ideological, or digital strategy.
2. Adapting to technological advancements is crucial; innovative nations often gain decisive advantages.
3. Intelligence and anticipation of enemy actions determine the success or failure of operations.

Conclusion

The Law of the Battlefield emphasizes the importance of preparation, adaptation, and innovation. Understanding and dominating the battlefield is critical for achieving geopolitical objectives in physical combat or non-traditional domains. This principle remains as relevant in modern cyber conflicts as in ancient wars.

References

1. Curtis, Glenn E. *Afghanistan: A Country Study*. Washington, DC: Library of Congress, 2008. https://www.loc.gov/item/2010292299/.

2. Doubler, Michael D. *Closing with the Enemy: How GIs Fought the War in Europe, 1944–1945*. Lawrence: University Press of Kansas, 1994. https://www.kansaspress.ku.edu/9780700612497.html.

3. Singer, Peter W. "The Predator Comes Home." *Foreign Affairs* 93, no. 3 (2014): 122–38. https://www.foreignaffairs.com/articles/united-states/2014-05-01/predator-comes-home.

4. Davis, Joshua. "The Secret War." *Wired*. August 21, 2007. https://www.wired.com/2007/08/ff-estonia/.

3. THE LAW OF PERCEPTION

SECTION 3: THE LAW OF PERCEPTION

Abstract

Perception often shapes geopolitical realities, influencing how nations are viewed and act on the global stage. *The Law of Perception* underscores the strategic importance of managing international narratives and shaping public opinion. Mechanisms of perception management in geopolitics are analyzed using historical and contemporary examples. Peer-reviewed research provides actionable insights for effective implementation.

Introduction

Perception is a critical dimension of power in geopolitics. How a nation or leader is perceived affects their ability to form alliances, deter adversaries, and influence global agendas. This law highlights that managing perception is not just a soft-power tactic but a strategic necessity in achieving long-term geopolitical objectives.

Key Components of The Law of Perception

1. The Role of Media and Communication

Media is a primary tool for shaping perceptions. Nations often leverage state-owned media, international press, and digital platforms to frame narratives favorably.

- **Case Study:** During the Cold War, the United States effectively utilized the Voice of America broadcasts to counter Soviet propaganda and promote democracy globally. Research in *The Historical Journal of Film, Radio, and Television* examines its impact on shaping public opinion in Eastern Europe (Patrick Major, "The Death of Koba: Stalin's Cult, Media and the Cold War in 1950s Britain," *The Historical Journal of Film, Radio, and Television* 34, no. 2 [2014]: 203–20, https://doi.org/10.1080/01439685.2014.879382).

2. Soft Power and Cultural Diplomacy

A nation's culture, values, and ideals contribute significantly to its global image. Leaders who understand this leverage cultural exchanges, education, and humanitarian aid to build positive perceptions.

- **Example:** China's Belt and Road Initiative includes cultural diplomacy efforts like Confucius Institutes to promote its language and culture, softening its image as an economic and geopolitical competitor (Joseph Nye, "Soft Power," *Foreign Policy* 80 [1990]: 153–71, https://www.foreignaffairs.com/articles/1990-10-01/soft-power).

3. Strategic Communication in Crises

In times of crisis, perception management becomes crucial. Leaders who communicate effectively can rally support and maintain international credibility.

- **Research Insight:** Studies on crisis communication during COVID-19 show that transparent, empathetic leadership improved government trust. See, for example, Amanda H. G. Neilson et al., "Trust in Crisis Communication: Exploring Public Perceptions of Transparency and Honesty in COVID-19 Messaging," *Journal of Communication* 72, no. 4 (2022): 521–41, https://doi.org/10.1093/joc/jqac025.

Application of The Law

1. Diplomatic Engagement

Managing perception in diplomatic efforts is critical. Leaders must project confidence and reliability to strengthen alliances and negotiate effectively.

2. Military Strategy

In military operations, controlling the narrative can be as important as battlefield victories. For example, the U.S. military's strategic communications during the Iraq War aimed to win hearts and minds, although its effectiveness was mixed.

3. Economic Influence

Nations also use economic initiatives to shape perceptions. The Marshall Plan post-WWII established the U.S. as a benevolent leader, fostering goodwill among European nations.

Lessons Learned

1. Perception is a reality in international relations. Failing to manage perception can undermine even the most robust strategies.

2. Transparency, consistency, and cultural diplomacy are vital tools for building and maintaining trust.

3. Leaders must proactively engage in narrative building, especially in a world increasingly shaped by social media and instantaneous communication.

Conclusion

The Law of Perception highlights that the success of geopolitical strategies often hinges on how they are perceived. Nations must understand and actively shape these perceptions to achieve their objectives. This principle serves as a cornerstone for understanding the interplay between reality and narrative in geopolitics.

References

1. Major, Patrick. "The Death of Koba: Stalin's Cult, Media and the Cold War in 1950s Britain." *The Historical Journal of Film, Radio, and Television* 34, no. 2 (2014): 203–20. https://doi.org/10.1080/01439685.2014.879382.

2. Nye, Joseph. "Soft Power." *Foreign Policy* 80 (1990): 153–71. https://www.foreignaffairs.com/articles/1990-10-01/soft-power.

3. Neilson, Amanda H. G., et al. "Trust in Crisis Communication: Exploring Public Perceptions of Transparency and Honesty in COVID-19 Messaging." *Journal of Communication* 72, no. 4 (2022): 521–41. https://doi.org/10.1093/joc/jqac025.

4. THE LAW OF FOCUS

SECTION 4: THE LAW OF FOCUS

Abstract

In geopolitics, focus is a critical determinant of strategic success. *The Law of Focus* asserts that nations must concentrate their efforts on a limited set of strategic objectives to maximize impact and resource efficiency. Historical and contemporary examples demonstrate the effectiveness of focused strategies. Peer-reviewed research and actionable insights highlight the critical role of focus in achieving geopolitical goals.

Introduction

Focus in geopolitics is about prioritization. Nations that disperse their resources across too many fronts often find themselves overextended, vulnerable, and unable to achieve their objectives. Conversely, a concentrated approach enables the efficient allocation of resources and a higher probability of success.

Key Components of The Law of Focus

1. Prioritizing Core Objectives

Successful strategies begin with clearly defined priorities. Nations must identify their most critical interests and allocate resources accordingly.

- **Case Study**: Post-World War II, the United States focused on rebuilding Western Europe through the Marshall Plan, which not only restored stability but also solidified its influence over the region (Michael Hogan, *The Marshall Plan: America, Britain, and the Reconstruction of Western Europe, 1947–1952* [Cambridge: Cambridge University Press, 1987], https://doi.org/10.1017/CBO9780511622136).

2. Avoiding Overextension

A lack of focus often leads to overextension, draining resources and creating vulnerabilities. Historical empires, such as Rome, provide cautionary tales of the dangers of spreading resources too thin.

- **Example:** The Roman Empire's overreach into distant territories strained its military and administrative capacities, ultimately contributing to its decline (Edward Gibbon, *The History of the Decline and Fall of the Roman Empire,* 1776, https://www.gutenberg.org/ebooks/731).

3. Concentration of Resources

Focusing resources on a specific goal amplifies a nation's capacity to achieve it. This principle is evident in modern military strategies, where concentrated efforts often determine success.

- **Research Insight:** A study on the Gulf War emphasizes how coalition forces' focused strategy on air superiority and rapid ground maneuvers secured a decisive victory (Richard Hallion, *Storm Over Iraq: Air Power and the Gulf War* [Washington, DC: Smithsonian Institution Press, 1992], https://archive.org/details/stormoveriraq00hall).

Application of The Law

1. Military Strategy

Focusing on a singular objective, such as capturing a key territory or disrupting an adversary's command structure, is often more effective than dispersing forces.

2. Economic Strategy

Nations that prioritize key industries for development, such as technology or energy, can achieve significant economic advantages. Consider China's focus on becoming a global leader in renewable energy technologies.

3. Diplomatic Strategy

Focused diplomacy allows nations to strengthen specific alliances or resolve critical conflicts without becoming overburdened. For example, the Camp David Accords focused on mediating peace between Egypt and Israel, creating a lasting impact.

Lessons Learned

1. Focus ensures that military, economic, or diplomatic resources are used effectively to achieve strategic objectives.
2. Overextension is a common pitfall for nations that fail to prioritize, often leading to strategic vulnerabilities.
3. Concentrated efforts in key areas can yield outsized results, establishing long-term influence and stability.

Conclusion

The Law of Focus underscores that success in geopolitics requires clear priorities and disciplined resource allocation. Nations that focus on their most critical objectives maximize their chances of success and establish a foundation for enduring influence and power. This principle is a cornerstone for understanding strategic efficiency in an increasingly complex global landscape.

References

1. Hogan, Michael. *The Marshall Plan: America, Britain, and the Reconstruction of Western Europe, 1947–1952.* Cambridge: Cambridge University Press, 1987. https://doi.org/10.1017/CBO9780511622136.

2. Gibbon, Edward. *The History of the Decline and Fall of the Roman Empire.* 1776. https://www.gutenberg.org/ebooks/731.

3. Hallion, Richard. *Storm Over Iraq: Air Power and the Gulf War.* Washington, DC: Smithsonian Institution Press, 1992. https://archive.org/details/stormoveriraq00hall.

5. THE LAW OF EXCLUSIVITY

SECTION 5: THE LAW OF EXCLUSIVITY

Abstract

Control over exclusive resources, technologies, or strategic positions often defines a nation's power and influence. *The Law of Exclusivity* posits that monopolizing critical assets can provide an unparalleled advantage in global politics. Historical and contemporary examples illustrate how exclusivity drives geopolitical strategies. Peer-reviewed research and actionable insights underscore its importance in maintaining and leveraging power.

Introduction

Exclusivity in geopolitics is the strategic control of critical resources, technologies, or knowledge that grants a nation a decisive advantage. Whether controlling natural resources, dominating technological innovation, or maintaining strategic geographic positions, exclusivity often determines a nation's ability to influence global events and protect its interests.

Key Components of The Law of Exclusivity

1. Resource Monopolization

Nations that dominate vital resources often wield significant global influence. Oil, rare earth elements, and water rights are examples of resources that confer power to their holders.

- **Case Study:** Saudi Arabia's control over vast oil reserves has positioned it as a key player in global energy markets and geopolitics. The founding of OPEC in 1960 exemplifies the use of exclusivity to consolidate power (Daniel Yergin, *The Prize: The Epic Quest for Oil, Money, and Power* [New York: Simon & Schuster, 1991], https://doi.org/10.1215/9780822356902-007).

2. Technological Domination

Control over cutting-edge technologies creates strategic leverage. The United States' dominance in semiconductor manufacturing and artificial intelligence underscores the role of exclusivity in maintaining global leadership.

- **Example:** Taiwan's TSMC (Taiwan Semiconductor Manufacturing Company) is the world's leading producer of advanced semiconductors, making Taiwan a critical player in global technology and geopolitics (Chris Miller, *Chip War: The Fight for the World's Most Critical Technology* [New York: Scribner, 2022], https://www.chip-war.com/).

3. Geographic Advantage

Strategic locations often serve as exclusive assets in global power struggles. Nations that control chokepoints like the Strait of Hormuz or the Suez Canal wield disproportionate influence over trade and military movements.

- **Research Insight**: The Suez Canal, controlled by Egypt, remains a critical artery for global trade. Its temporary closure in 2021 due to the *Ever Given* incident demonstrated its importance to the global economy (Yasmin El-Geressi, "How the Suez Canal Blockage Affected Global Trade," *The Maritime Executive*, April 1, 2021, https://www.maritime-executive.com/article/how-the-suez-canal-blockage-affected-global-trade).

Application of The Law

1. Economic Leverage

Resource-rich nations can use exclusivity to negotiate favorable terms in international agreements. For example, Russia's control over European natural gas supplies has historically given it significant bargaining power.

2. Technological Leadership

Nations that invest in and protect exclusive technologies maintain a competitive edge in the civilian and military sectors. The race for 5G technology illustrates the criticality of technological exclusivity.

3. Military Strategy

Control of exclusive geographic locations often determines the outcome of military conflicts. The Allied control of Normandy during D-Day is a historic example of leveraging geographic exclusivity.

Lessons Learned

1. Nations that control exclusive resources, technologies, or strategic locations wield significant influence over global politics.
2. Overdependence on exclusive assets can create vulnerabilities, as reliance often leads to geopolitical tensions.
3. Exclusivity is dynamic; nations must continuously innovate and protect their exclusive advantages to maintain relevance.

Conclusion

The Law of Exclusivity demonstrates that monopolizing critical assets—whether natural, technological, or geographic—provides nations with a unique advantage in the global arena. However, maintaining exclusivity requires vigilance, strategic foresight, and adaptability in the face of evolving geopolitical challenges.

References

1. Yergin, Daniel. *The Prize: The Epic Quest for Oil, Money, and Power.* New York: Simon & Schuster, 1991. https://doi.org/10.1215/9780822356902-007.

2. Miller, Chris. *Chip War: The Fight for the World's Most Critical Technology.* New York: Scribner, 2022. https://www.chipwar.com/.

3. El-Geressi, Yasmin. "How the Suez Canal Blockage Affected Global Trade." *The Maritime Executive.* April 1, 2021. https://www.maritime-executive.com/article/how-the-suez-canal-blockage-affected-global-trade.

6. THE LAW OF DUALITY

SECTION 6: THE LAW OF DUALITY

Abstract

Geopolitical strategy is often a balancing act where every decision has both positive and negative consequences. *The Law of Duality* emphasizes the need for nations to weigh the trade-offs of their actions and find equilibrium between competing interests.

Introduction

In geopolitics, success is rarely achieved without cost. For every advantage gained, there is often a corresponding disadvantage that must be managed. *The Law of Duality* highlights this interplay, urging leaders to consider the full spectrum of consequences before committing to a course of action.

Key Components of The Law of Duality

1. Balancing Security and Freedom

Nations often face the dilemma of ensuring security while preserving individual freedoms. Striking the right balance is crucial for maintaining public trust and social stability.

- **Case Study:** Post-9/11, the United States enacted the Patriot Act to enhance security but faced criticism for infringing on civil liberties. Scholarly analyses reveal how this trade-off influenced public perception and policy effectiveness (Richard A. Posner, "Security Versus Civil Liberties," *The Atlantic Monthly*, December 2001, https://www.theatlantic.com/magazine/archive/2001/12/security-versus-civil-liberties/302355/).

2. Economic Growth vs. Environmental Sustainability

Rapid industrialization often drives economic growth but at a significant environmental cost. Nations must balance immediate economic gains with long-term ecological health.

- **Example:** China's economic rise has come with severe environmental challenges, including air and water pollution. The government's recent pivot toward renewable energy illustrates an effort to manage this duality (Yuan Xu, "China's Environmental Policy,"

Annual Review of Environment and Resources 39 [2014]: 321–44, https://doi.org/10.1146/annurev-environ-031913-102620).

3. Military Expansion and Diplomacy

While military expansion can strengthen national defense and global influence, it often strains diplomatic relations and escalates tensions.

- **Research Insight:** NATO's eastward expansion post-Cold War strengthened security for member states but heightened tensions with Russia, contributing to the ongoing Ukraine conflict (John J. Mearsheimer, "Why the Ukraine Crisis Is the West's Fault," *Foreign Affairs* 93, no. 5 [2014]: 77–89, https://www.foreignaffairs.com/articles/russia-fsu/2014-08-18/why-ukraine-crisis-west-s-fault).

Application of The Law

1. **National Security Policy**
   Leaders must carefully navigate dualities in policies like mass surveillance, where the benefits of enhanced security must be weighed against the erosion of privacy rights.

2. **Economic Strategy**
   Developing economies often prioritize industrial growth over environmental sustainability, but long-term planning requires investment in green technologies to mitigate negative impacts.

3. **International Relations**
   The duality of military power and diplomacy necessitates a balanced approach. Nations that over-rely on force risk alienating allies and provoking adversaries.

Lessons Learned

1. Every strategic action involves trade-offs that must be anticipated and managed.

2. Failing to address dualities often leads to long-term instability, even when short-term goals are achieved.

3. Leaders must adopt a holistic perspective, considering immediate outcomes and future implications.

Conclusion

The Law of Duality underscores the inherent trade-offs in geopolitical strategy. By understanding and managing these dualities, nations can achieve their objectives while minimizing unintended consequences. This principle serves as a reminder that every decision carries both opportunity and risk.

References

1. Posner, Richard A. "Security Versus Civil Liberties." *The Atlantic Monthly*. December 2001. https://www.theatlantic.com/magazine/archive/2001/12/security-versus-civil-liberties/302355/.

2. Xu, Yuan. "China's Environmental Policy." *Annual Review of Environment and Resources* 39 (2014): 321–44. https://doi.org/10.1146/annurev-environ-031913-102620.

3. Mearsheimer, John J. "Why the Ukraine Crisis Is the West's Fault." *Foreign Affairs* 93, no. 5 (2014): 77–89. https://www.foreignaffairs.com/articles/russia-fsu/2014-08-18/why-ukraine-crisis-west-s-fault.

7. THE LAW OF THE OPPOSITE

SECTION 7: THE LAW OF THE OPPOSITE

Abstract

In geopolitics, adopting strategies opposite to those of rivals can create significant advantages. *The Law of the Opposite* highlights the importance of differentiation in strategic planning.

Introduction

The ability to think and act contrarily to opponents has often defined success in geopolitical contests. By diverging from conventional approaches, nations can exploit weaknesses in their rivals' strategies. This principle encourages innovation and adaptability in the face of evolving challenges.

Key Components of The Law of the Opposite

1. Strategic Differentiation

Differentiation allows nations to focus on their strengths while countering their rivals' weaknesses.

- **Case Study:** During the Cold War, the United States emphasized technological innovation, such as the Space Race, while the Soviet Union focused on military expansion. This contrast allowed the U.S. to project soft power and gain a competitive edge in global influence (Walter A. McDougall, *The Heavens, and the Earth: A Political History of the Space Age* [Baltimore: Johns Hopkins University Press, 1997], https://jhupbooks.press.jhu.edu/title/heavens-and-earth).

2. Economic Opposition

Adopting contrasting economic policies can also yield advantages. For example, open-market policies can contrast sharply with rivals' state-controlled economies, attracting foreign investment.

- **Example:** In the 1980s, the Reagan Administration's emphasis on deregulation and free-market capitalism starkly contrasted with the Soviet Union's centrally planned economy. This differentiation contributed to the eventual collapse of the Soviet economy (Francis Fukuyama, *The End of History and the Last Man* [New York: Free Press, 1992], https://www.simonandschuster.com/books/The-End-of-History-and-the-Last-Man/Francis-Fukuyama/9780743284554).

3. Military Strategy

In conflicts, adopting unorthodox strategies often leads to success.

- **Research Insight**: During the Vietnam War, the North Vietnamese relied on guerrilla tactics to counter U.S. conventional warfare strategies, effectively leveraging asymmetry to their advantage (Andrew F. Krepinevich Jr., *The Army and Vietnam* [Baltimore: Johns Hopkins University Press, 1986], https://jhupbooks.press.jhu.edu/title/army-and-vietnam).

Application of The Law

1. **Diplomatic Strategy**
   Diplomatic approaches that diverge from rivals' tactics, such as emphasizing multilateralism versus unilateralism, can strengthen alliances and isolate adversaries.

2. **Technological Development**
   Pursuing areas of innovation ignored by rivals creates competitive advantages. For example, focusing on renewable energy while competitors prioritize fossil fuels can establish leadership in future markets.

3. **Cultural Influence**
   Promoting cultural values contrary to rival ideologies fosters global appeal. The U.S.'s promotion of individual freedoms and democracy starkly contrasted Soviet collectivism, enhancing its soft power during the Cold War.

Lessons Learned

1. Differentiation allows nations to capitalize on rivals' weaknesses while reinforcing their own strengths.

2. Contrasting approaches can attract allies, improve global standing, and increase competitiveness.

3. The Law of the Opposite requires foresight and adaptability to anticipate rival strategies and adjust accordingly.

Conclusion

The Law of the Opposite illustrates the value of divergence in geopolitics. By adopting strategies that contrast with those of rivals, nations can achieve advantages that would otherwise be unattainable. This principle underscores the importance of innovation, flexibility, and strategic foresight in global strategy.

References

1. McDougall, Walter A. *The Heavens and the Earth: A Political History of the Space Age*. Baltimore: Johns Hopkins University Press, 1997. https://jhupbooks.press.jhu.edu/title/heavens-and-earth.

2. Fukuyama, Francis. *The End of History and the Last Man*. New York: Free Press, 1992. https://www.simonandschuster.com/books/The-End-of-History-and-the-Last-Man/Francis-Fukuyama/9780743284554.

3. Krepinevich, Andrew F. Jr. *The Army and Vietnam*. Baltimore: Johns Hopkins University Press, 1986. https://jhupbooks.press.jhu.edu/title/army-and-vietnam.

SECTION 8: THE LAW OF DIVISION

Abstract

Geopolitical landscapes are often fragmented into spheres of influence, with power concentrated among key players. *The Law of Division* underscores the importance of understanding and navigating these divisions to maintain stability and achieve strategic objectives.

Introduction

The division is inherent in geopolitics. Nations, regions, and alliances often divide along cultural, political, economic, and ideological lines. *The Law of Division* highlights the necessity for nations to understand these fault lines, as failing to account for them can lead to missteps or conflicts. Conversely, leveraging these divisions can enhance influence and strategic positioning.

Key Components of The Law of Division

1. Spheres of Influence

Global politics often revolves around spheres of influence, where dominant powers control specific regions.

- **Case Study**: The Cold War exemplified a bipolar division, with the United States and the Soviet Union competing for global influence. The division of Germany into East and West serves as a microcosm of this larger dynamic (Melvyn P. Leffler, *For the Soul of Mankind: The United States, the Soviet Union, and the Cold War* [New York: Hill and Wang, 2007], https://us.macmillan.com/books/9780809097173/forthesoulofmankind).

2. Ethnic and Cultural Divisions

Ethnic and cultural divisions often shape nations' geopolitical strategies, leading to opportunities and challenges.

- **Example**: The dissolution of Yugoslavia in the 1990s revealed the fragility of forced unification, with ethnic divisions fueling violent conflicts and geopolitical shifts (Susan L. Woodward, *Balkan Tragedy: Chaos and Dissolution After the Cold War*

[Washington, DC: Brookings Institution Press, 1995], https://www.brookings.edu/book/balkan-tragedy/).

3. Economic and Ideological Divisions

Economic disparities and ideological differences frequently drive global divisions, influencing trade, alliances, and conflicts.

- **Research Insight:** The ongoing divide between developed and developing nations in trade agreements, such as during World Trade Organization negotiations, highlights the impact of economic division on international policymaking (Amrita Narlikar, *The World Trade Organization: A Very Short Introduction* [Oxford: Oxford University Press, 2005], https://global.oup.com/academic/product/the-world-trade-organization-a-very-short-introduction-9780192806086).

Application of The Law

1. **Regional Strategy**
   Nations must navigate regional divisions to secure their interests. For example, China leverages divisions within ASEAN to prevent unified opposition to its South China Sea claims.

2. **Conflict Resolution**
   Understanding divisions is critical for resolving conflicts. Efforts to mediate peace in the Middle East often fail due to an inadequate understanding of sectarian and cultural divides.

3. **Alliance Formation**
   Divisions can be used strategically to form alliances, as seen in NATO's efforts to bring Eastern European nations into its fold following the Cold War.

Lessons Learned

1. Recognizing and understanding divisions in geopolitics is essential for formulating effective strategies.

2. Exploiting divisions can enhance influence, but overreliance on divisive strategies risks long-term instability.

3. Bridging divisions often requires nuanced diplomacy, cultural sensitivity, and long-term investment in trust-building.

Conclusion

The Law of Division underscores that fragmentation is a defining characteristic of geopolitics. Nations can secure their interests and maintain stability by understanding and navigating these divisions. However, leveraging divisions requires careful management to avoid exacerbating conflicts or alienating key stakeholders.

References

1. Leffler, Melvyn P. *For the Soul of Mankind: The United States, the Soviet Union, and the Cold War.* New York: Hill and Wang, 2007. https://us.macmillan.com/books/9780809097173/forthesoulofmankind.

2. Woodward, Susan L. *Balkan Tragedy: Chaos and Dissolution After the Cold War.* Washington, DC: Brookings Institution Press, 1995. https://www.brookings.edu/book/balkan-tragedy/.

3. Narlikar, Amrita. *The World Trade Organization: A Very Short Introduction.* Oxford: Oxford University Press, 2005. https://global.oup.com/academic/product/the-world-trade-organization-a-very-short-introduction-9780192806086.

SECTION 9: THE LAW OF PERSPECTIVE

Abstract

A long-term perspective is essential for sustainable success in geopolitics. *The Law of Perspective* asserts that nations and leaders must anticipate future trends and challenges to maintain influence and stability.

Introduction

In geopolitics, short-term gains often come at the cost of long-term stability. *The Law of Perspective* emphasizes the importance of foresight in crafting policies and strategies. Leaders prioritizing a broader temporal horizon are better equipped to manage emerging challenges, seize opportunities, and leave lasting legacies.

Key Components of The Law of Perspective

1. Anticipating Trends

Successful leaders identify and adapt to emerging trends, positioning their nations for future advantages.

- **Case Study:** The Marshall Plan was not just about rebuilding Europe after World War II; it anticipated the geopolitical need to prevent Soviet expansion and ensure U.S. influence in the region (Michael Hogan, *The Marshall Plan: America, Britain, and the Reconstruction of Western Europe, 1947–1952* [Cambridge: Cambridge University Press, 1987], https://doi.org/10.1017/CBO9780511622136).

2. Balancing Immediate Needs with Long-Term Goals

Leaders must address current challenges without losing sight of overarching objectives.

- **Example:** Singapore's founding Prime Minister, Lee Kuan Yew, implemented policies to transition the country from a struggling port city to a global economic hub, demonstrating a remarkable focus on long-term outcomes (Lee Kuan Yew, *From Third World to First: The Singapore Story* [New York: HarperCollins, 2000], https://www.harpercollins.com/products/from-third-world-to-first-lee-kuan-yew).

3. Investing in Future Resilience

Infrastructure, education, and innovation investments are critical to sustaining influence and stability over time.

- **Research Insight**: A study on Japan's post-war reconstruction highlights how early investments in education and industrial infrastructure laid the foundation for its rapid economic recovery (Chalmers Johnson, *MITI and the Japanese Miracle: The Growth of Industrial Policy, 1925–1975* [Stanford: Stanford University Press, 1982], https://www.sup.org/books/title/?id=2865).

Application of The Law

1. **Economic Strategy**
   Long-term planning for renewable energy, technology, and education secures sustainable economic growth. For example, Germany's Energiewende (energy transition) reflects its forward-thinking approach to reducing dependence on fossil fuels.

2. **Diplomatic Strategy**
   Nations must cultivate alliances and partnerships with a long-term vision, prioritizing trust and mutual benefits over short-term gains.

3. **Military Strategy**
   Modernizing military capabilities and adapting to new domains like cyberspace ensures readiness for future conflicts.

Lessons Learned

1. A long-term perspective enables nations to anticipate and mitigate future risks while capitalizing on emerging opportunities.

2. Leaders must balance immediate actions with the overarching vision to avoid undermining future goals.

3. Infrastructure, education, and innovation investments are crucial for maintaining long-term influence and stability.

Conclusion

The Law of Perspective emphasizes that strategic foresight is a cornerstone of effective geopolitical leadership. Nations prioritizing long-term planning are better equipped to navigate the complexities of global politics, ensuring resilience and relevance in an ever-changing world.

References

1. Hogan, Michael. *The Marshall Plan: America, Britain, and the Reconstruction of Western Europe, 1947–1952.* Cambridge: Cambridge University Press, 1987. https://doi.org/10.1017/CBO9780511622136.

2. Lee, Kuan Yew. *From Third World to First: The Singapore Story.* New York: HarperCollins, 2000. https://www.harpercollins.com/products/from-third-world-to-first-lee-kuan-yew.

3. Johnson, Chalmers. *MITI and the Japanese Miracle: The Growth of Industrial Policy, 1925–1975.* Stanford: Stanford University Press, 1982. https://www.sup.org/books/title/?id=2865.

SECTION 10: THE LAW OF LINE EXTENSION

Abstract

In geopolitics, overextension of power and influence often leads to vulnerabilities and decline. *The Law of Line Extension* highlights the dangers of thinly spreading resources and attention, advocating for strategic focus and consolidation.

Introduction

The expansion of influence, whether territorial, economic, or ideological, is often a sign of strength. However, overextension—expanding beyond sustainable limits—frequently results in strategic vulnerability and loss of control. *The Law of Line Extension* reminds leaders that restraint and focus are as necessary as ambition in sustaining power.

Key Components of The Law of Line Extension

1. The Risks of Overreach

Expanding too rapidly or into areas beyond a nation's management capacity creates vulnerabilities.

- **Case Study:** The Roman Empire's overextension into distant and diverse territories strained its administrative and military resources, contributing to its eventual fall (Edward Gibbon, *The History of the Decline and Fall of the Roman Empire*, 1776, https://www.gutenberg.org/ebooks/731).

2. Sustainable Growth and Influence

Sustainable expansion focuses on consolidating gains rather than pursuing unchecked growth.

- **Example:** Post-World War II, the United States expanded its influence through carefully managed alliances like NATO, focusing on shared defense rather than unilateral dominance (Mark Mazower, *Governing the World: The History of an Idea* [New York: Penguin, 2012], https://www.penguinrandomhouse.com/books/309127/governing-the-world-by-mark-mazower/).

3. Economic Overextension

Nations that overextend their economic commitments, such as through excessive debt or unsustainable development projects, risk financial collapse.

- **Research Insight:** Japan's economic stagnation in the 1990s, following its rapid expansion in the 1980s, illustrates the consequences of overinvestment and insufficient focus on domestic market resilience (Richard Katz, *Japan: The System That Soured* [New York: M.E. Sharpe, 1998], https://www.routledge.com/Japan-The-System-That-Soured-1st-Edition/Katz/p/book/9781563248985).

Application of The Law

1. **Territorial Expansion**
   Nations must ensure that territorial acquisitions are defensible and manageable. The British Empire's gradual decolonization demonstrated an acknowledgment of overreach and an attempt to recalibrate influence.

2. **Economic Strategy**
   Avoiding overextension requires balancing global investments with domestic priorities. For example, China's Belt and Road Initiative risks overextending its financial and diplomatic resources, raising concerns about sustainability.

3. **Military Strategy**
   Overcommitting military resources across multiple fronts can lead to strategic failures. The Soviet Union's involvement in Afghanistan is a stark example of the dangers of military overreach.

Lessons Learned

1. Expansion should be strategic and sustainable, ensuring that resources can support new commitments.

2. Consolidation is as important as growth; nations must periodically focus on strengthening their existing assets and influence.

3. Overextension often results in vulnerabilities that adversaries can exploit, leading to strategic decline.

Conclusion

The Law of Line Extension underscores that less is often more in geopolitics. Sustainable growth, strategic consolidation, and a clear understanding of capacity are crucial for long-term success. Nations that manage their ambitions wisely are better positioned to maintain influence and stability over time.

References

1. Gibbon, Edward. *The History of the Decline and Fall of the Roman Empire.* 1776. https://www.gutenberg.org/ebooks/731.

2. Mazower, Mark. *Governing the World: The History of an Idea.* New York: Penguin, 2012. https://www.penguinrandomhouse.com/books/309127/governing-the-world-by-mark-mazower/.

3. Katz, Richard. *Japan: The System That Soured.* New York: M.E. Sharpe, 1998. https://www.routledge.com/Japan-The-System-That-Soured-1st-Edition/Katz/p/book/9781563248985.

SECTION 11: THE LAW OF SACRIFICE

Abstract

In geopolitics, achieving long-term strategic goals often requires short-term sacrifices. *The Law of Sacrifice* posits that nations must make difficult choices to allocate resources effectively, prioritize critical objectives, and maintain focus.

Introduction

Sacrifice is an inherent component of strategic planning. Leaders must recognize that resources are finite and that pursuing every goal simultaneously dilutes effectiveness. *The Law of Sacrifice* underscores the need for disciplined decision-making, where short-term concessions enable long-term gains.

Key Components of The Law of Sacrifice

1. Prioritizing Long-Term Goals Over Immediate Gratification

Sacrifice often involves delaying rewards to achieve greater long-term outcomes.

- **Case Study**: Post-World War II, Germany sacrificed immediate national sovereignty by accepting Allied occupation and integration into the Marshall Plan. This decision laid the groundwork for its economic recovery and long-term stability (Michael Hogan, *The Marshall Plan: America, Britain, and the Reconstruction of Western Europe, 1947–1952* [Cambridge: Cambridge University Press, 1987], https://doi.org/10.1017/CBO9780511622136).

2. Military Sacrifice for Strategic Positioning

In military strategy, sacrificing less critical positions to protect vital assets or gain a strategic advantage is a recurring theme.

- **Example**: During World War II, the Soviet Union's scorched-earth policy involved destroying resources to deny them to advancing German forces. This sacrifice proved crucial in blunting the Nazi invasion (Richard Overy, *Russia's War: A History of the*

Soviet Effort: 1941–1945 [New York: Penguin, 1998], https://www.penguinrandomhouse.com/books/311474/russias-war-by-richard-overy/).

3. Economic Sacrifices for Future Prosperity

Economic reforms often require short-term sacrifices, such as austerity measures or restructuring, to stabilize economies and enable growth.

- **Research Insight**: In the late 20th century, South Korea implemented economic policies prioritizing industrial development over consumer goods production. This sacrifice transformed it into a global manufacturing powerhouse (Alice H. Amsden, *Asia's Next Giant: South Korea and Late Industrialization* [Oxford: Oxford University Press, 1989], https://global.oup.com/academic/product/asias-next-giant-9780195076035).

Application of The Law

1. **Diplomatic Strategy**
   Nations may sacrifice unilateral decision-making by participating in multilateral agreements to secure long-term stability and alliances.

2. **Economic Policy**
   Sacrificing short-term consumption for infrastructure, education, or technology investment pays dividends in sustained growth and competitiveness.

3. **Military Strategy**
   Military commanders often sacrifice smaller units or territories to preserve larger strategic objectives, as seen in the Allied strategy of focusing on Europe before fully engaging in the Pacific during WWII.

Lessons Learned

1. Sacrifice is not a sign of weakness but a calculated decision to prioritize long-term objectives.

2. Leaders must communicate the reasons for sacrifice to maintain public support and organizational morale.

3. Failing to sacrifice when necessary often results in overextension or failure to achieve critical goals.

Conclusion

The Law of Sacrifice emphasizes the importance of disciplined decision-making in geopolitics. Nations can achieve sustainable success by prioritizing long-term objectives and making short-term sacrifices. Leaders who master this principle enhance their capacity to navigate complexity and maintain strategic focus.

References

1. Hogan, Michael. *The Marshall Plan: America, Britain, and the Reconstruction of Western Europe, 1947–1952.* Cambridge: Cambridge University Press, 1987. https://doi.org/10.1017/CBO9780511622136.

2. Overy, Richard. *Russia's War: A History of the Soviet Effort: 1941–1945.* New York: Penguin, 1998. https://www.penguinrandomhouse.com/books/311474/russias-war-by-richard-overy/.

3. Amsden, Alice H. *Asia's Next Giant: South Korea and Late Industrialization.* Oxford: Oxford University Press, 1989. https://global.oup.com/academic/product/asias-next-giant-9780195076035.

SECTION 12: THE LAW OF ADAPTABILITY

Abstract

In an ever-changing geopolitical landscape, adaptability is a cornerstone of success. *The Law of Adaptability* emphasizes the importance of flexibility, innovation, and responsiveness in national and organizational strategies.

Introduction

The global stage constantly changes, influenced by evolving technologies, shifting alliances, and emerging threats. Success belongs to those who adapt quickly and effectively. *The Law of Adaptability* underscores the need for nations and leaders to anticipate changes, adjust strategies, and seize opportunities in uncertain environments.

Key Components of The Law of Adaptability

1. Flexibility in Strategy

Rigid adherence to outdated strategies often leads to failure. Successful leaders recognize the need for flexibility in the face of new information or shifting circumstances.

- **Case Study:** The U.S. pivot to Asia under the Obama Administration marked a strategic adjustment to address the rise of China as a global power, demonstrating adaptability in foreign policy (Kurt M. Campbell, *The Pivot: The Future of American Statecraft in Asia* [New York: Twelve, 2016], https://www.hachettebookgroup.com/titles/kurt-campbell/the-pivot/9781455568976/).

2. Technological Innovation

Adapting to technological advancements is essential for maintaining relevance and competitiveness.

- **Example:** Israel's development of the Iron Dome missile defense system exemplifies adaptability in addressing evolving security threats, leveraging cutting-edge technology to counter asymmetrical warfare (Yaakov Katz and Amir Bohbot, *The Weapon Wizards: How Israel Became a High-Tech Military Superpower* [New York: St. Martin's Press, 2017], https://us.macmillan.com/books/9781250118744/theweaponwizards).

3. Economic Adaptation

Nations that adapt to global economic trends thrive, while those resistant to change often stagnate.

- **Research Insight:** Germany's shift to renewable energy through its Energiewende policy demonstrates economic and environmental adaptability in transitioning from traditional fossil fuels to sustainable energy (Claus Leggewie and Marcel Siepmann, *Energiewende: Germany's Transition to Renewable Energy* [Cambridge: Polity Press, 2019], https://politybooks.com/energiewende-germanys-transition-to-renewable-energy/).

Application of The Law

1. **Military Strategy**
   Modernizing military capabilities and adopting new technologies ensures readiness for unconventional conflicts, such as cyber and drone warfare.

2. **Economic Policy**
   Governments must adjust fiscal and trade policies to respond to global economic shifts, including emerging industries and digital economies.

3. **Diplomatic Relations**
   Flexibility in alliances and negotiations is critical. For instance, nations must adapt to multipolarity by engaging with diverse partners rather than relying solely on traditional partnerships.

Lessons Learned

1. Adaptability is a prerequisite for survival and success in dynamic geopolitical environments.

2. Leaders who embrace change and innovation position their nations to capitalize on emerging opportunities.

3. Resistance to change often results in decline, as exemplified by historical failures to address technological or economic disruptions.

Conclusion

The Law of Adaptability emphasizes that flexibility and innovation are indispensable in a world of constant change. Nations and leaders adapting to shifting circumstances secure their place in the global arena, while those who cling to outdated strategies risk irrelevance.

References

1. Campbell, Kurt M. *The Pivot: The Future of American Statecraft in Asia.* New York: Twelve, 2016. https://www.hachettebookgroup.com/titles/kurt-campbell/the-pivot/9781455568976/.

2. Katz, Yaakov, and Amir Bohbot. *The Weapon Wizards: How Israel Became a High-Tech Military Superpower.* New York: St. Martin's Press, 2017. https://us.macmillan.com/books/9781250118744/theweaponwizards.

3. Leggewie, Claus, and Marcel Siepmann. *Energiewende: Germany's Transition to Renewable Energy.* Cambridge: Polity Press, 2019. https://politybooks.com/energiewende-germanys-transition-to-renewable-energy/.

SECTION 13: THE LAW OF ALLIANCES

Abstract

The Law of Alliances underscores the importance of forging strategic partnerships to achieve mutual benefits, amplify strength, and mitigate shared risks. In geopolitics, alliances have been pivotal in shaping military victories, economic collaborations, and diplomatic achievements.

Introduction

Alliances are formal or informal agreements between nations or groups that seek to achieve shared objectives by pooling resources, knowledge, or influence. From military coalitions to trade partnerships, alliances have been instrumental in addressing common threats and fostering collaboration.

Key Components of The Law of Alliances

1. **Mutual Benefit**
   Successful alliances thrive on shared interests and benefits for all parties involved.
   - *Example*: NATO's collective defense principle, where member states benefit from mutual security, exemplifies this concept (Kay 1998).
2. **Strength in Unity**
   Alliances enable nations to amplify their power by combining resources and capabilities.
   - *Case Study*: The Allied Powers during World War II demonstrated the strategic advantage of uniting against a common enemy, leading to the defeat of Axis forces (Beevor 2012).
3. **Balancing Power**
   Alliances are often formed to counterbalance the influence of rival powers, ensuring no single entity dominates.
   - *Modern Example*: The Quadrilateral Security Dialogue (Quad), involving the U.S., Japan, India, and Australia, aims to balance China's growing influence in the Indo-Pacific region (Green 2021).

Application of the Law

- **Military Strategy:** Military alliances like NATO provide collective defense and a unified response to aggression.
- **Economic Strategy:** Trade alliances such as the European Union (EU) enhance financial stability and growth through shared markets and policies (Moravcsik 1998).
- **Diplomatic Strategy:** Strategic partnerships enable nations to advance shared geopolitical interests, such as combating climate change or terrorism.
    - *Example:* The Five Eyes intelligence-sharing alliance among the U.S., UK, Canada, Australia, and New Zealand enhances global security (Aldrich 2012).

Lessons Learned

1. **Foster Trust Among Members:** Trust is the cornerstone of effective alliances; without it, partnerships are prone to failure.
2. **Adapt to Evolving Needs:** Alliances must remain flexible to address emerging challenges and opportunities.
3. **Avoid Overdependence:** While alliances amplify strength, overreliance on partners can undermine national autonomy.
4. **Prioritize Common Interests:** Alliances succeed when members align on shared goals, minimizing internal conflicts.

Conclusion

The Law of Alliances illustrates that collaboration is a force multiplier in geopolitics. By leveraging shared strengths and addressing common threats, alliances can secure peace, stability, and prosperity. However, the success of partnerships depend on trust, adaptability, and the pursuit of mutual benefit.

References

1. Aldrich, Richard J. *GCHQ: The Uncensored Story of Britain's Most Secret Intelligence Agency.* London: HarperCollins, 2012.
2. Beevor, Antony. *The Second World War.* London: Weidenfeld & Nicolson, 2012.
3. Green, Michael. *By More Than Providence: Grand Strategy and American Power in the Asia Pacific Since 1783.* New York: Columbia University Press, 2021.
4. Kay, Sean. *NATO and the Future of European Security.* Lanham, MD: Rowman & Littlefield, 1998.
5. Moravcsik, Andrew. "Preferences and Power in the European Community: A Liberal Intergovernmentalism Approach." *Journal of Common Market Studies* 31, no. 4 (1998): 473–524.

SECTION 14: THE LAW OF SOVEREIGNTY

Abstract

The Law of Sovereignty underscores the importance of a nation's ability to govern itself, control its resources, and make decisions without external interference. This principle, originating from the Peace of Westphalia (1648), remains central to geopolitical stability.

Introduction

Sovereignty is a fundamental concept in international relations, encapsulating a nation's control over its territory, resources, and governance. While rooted in historical precedents like the Peace of Westphalia, sovereignty today faces challenges from globalization, transnational threats, and foreign interventions.

Key Components of The Law of Sovereignty

1. **Territorial Integrity**
   Control over defined borders and territory is the foundation of sovereignty.
   - *Example*: Russia's annexation of Crimea in 2014 violated Ukraine's sovereignty and was widely condemned by the international community (Mearsheimer 2014). Available at: https://www.foreignaffairs.com/articles/russia-fsu/2014-08-18/why-ukraine-crisis-west-s-fault.
2. **Non-Interference**
   Sovereignty implies the right to govern without external interference.
   - *Case Study*: The Syrian Civil War saw significant violations of sovereignty through interventions by foreign powers (Weiss 2014). Available at: https://www.wiley.com/en-us/Humanitarian+Intervention%3A+Ideas+in+Action.
3. **Economic Sovereignty**
   The ability to control economic policies and resources is a key aspect of sovereignty.
   - *Modern Example*: International sanctions on Venezuela highlight tensions between sovereignty and global accountability (Pape 1997). Available at: https://www.mitpressjournals.org/doi/10.1162/isec.22.2.90.

Application of the Law

- **Geopolitical Strategy:** Nations defend sovereignty through alliances, military strength, and diplomacy. Taiwan, for instance, relies on U.S. support to maintain its sovereignty amid Chinese pressures (Bush 2013). Available at: https://www.brookings.edu/book/uncharted-strait/.

- **Economic Strategy:** Saudi Arabia asserts sovereignty over its oil resources through state-controlled Saudi Aramco (Gause 2015). Available at: https://www.cambridge.org/core/books/international-relations-of-the-persian-gulf.

- **Legal Strategy:** Disputes over sovereignty in the South China Sea demonstrate the use of international legal frameworks to assert territorial claims (Kaplan 2014). Available at: https://www.randomhousebooks.com/books/222207/.

Lessons Learned

1. **Balance Sovereignty and Globalization:** Nations must navigate the trade-offs between sovereignty and international collaboration.

2. **Defend Sovereignty with Strength:** Robust military, legal, and economic systems are essential for maintaining sovereignty.

3. **Respect Global Norms:** Adherence to international laws ensures sovereignty is recognized and protected globally.

4. **Adapt to Transnational Challenges:** Sovereignty must evolve to address climate change, cyber threats, and pandemics, which often transcend national boundaries.

Conclusion

The Law of Sovereignty remains a cornerstone of geopolitics, safeguarding national identity and stability. Modern challenges demand a nuanced approach, balancing sovereignty with the imperatives of globalization and international cooperation. By doing so, nations can protect their autonomy while addressing shared global challenges.

References

1. Bush, Richard C. *Uncharted Strait: The Future of China-Taiwan Relations.* Washington, DC: Brookings Institution Press, 2013. Available at: https://www.brookings.edu/book/uncharted-strait/.

2. Gause, F. Gregory. *The International Relations of the Persian Gulf.* Cambridge: Cambridge University Press, 2015. Available at: https://www.cambridge.org/core/books/international-relations-of-the-persian-gulf.

3. Kaplan, Robert D. *Asia's Cauldron: The South China Sea and the End of a Stable Pacific.* New York: Random House, 2014. Available at: https://www.randomhousebooks.com/books/222207/.

4. Mearsheimer, John J. "Why the Ukraine Crisis Is the West's Fault." *Foreign Affairs* 93, no. 5 (2014): 77–89. Available at: https://www.foreignaffairs.com/articles/russia-fsu/2014-08-18/why-ukraine-crisis-west-s-fault.

5. Pape, Robert A. "Why Economic Sanctions Do Not Work." *International Security* 22, no. 2 (1997): 90–136. Available at: https://www.mitpressjournals.org/doi/10.1162/isec.22.2.90.

6. Weiss, Thomas G. *Humanitarian Intervention: Ideas in Action.* 2nd ed. Cambridge: Polity, 2014. Available at: https://www.wiley.com/en-us/Humanitarian+Intervention%3A+Ideas+in+Action.

SECTION 15: THE LAW OF BALANCE

Abstract
The Law of Balance underscores the necessity of equilibrium in national strategy, particularly in maintaining stability across political, economic, military, and social domains. Nations prioritizing balance are better equipped to sustain power, manage crises, and adapt to global challenges.

Introduction

Balance is a guiding principle in geopolitics, ensuring nations avoid extremes that could lead to instability or overreach. By achieving equilibrium across key sectors, states can effectively manage their resources, secure long-term stability, and adapt to an evolving global order. The Law of Balance examines how this principle operates and impacts geopolitical success.

Key Components of The Law of Balance

1. **Political Balance**
   A nation's internal stability depends on a well-balanced political system that avoids authoritarianism or excessive fragmentation.

   - *Example*: Switzerland's political neutrality and decentralized governance have contributed to its long-term stability (Linder 2010).

2. **Economic Balance**
   Economic policies must balance growth, sustainability, and equity to ensure resilience against external shocks.

   - *Case Study*: Germany's post-reunification strategy balanced market-driven reforms with social safety nets, creating a robust economy (Streeck 1997).

3. **Military Balance**
   Balancing military strength with diplomatic engagement prevents overmilitarization and fosters global cooperation.

   - *Modern Example*: The U.S. employs a balance between hard power (military strength) and soft power (diplomacy and cultural influence) in its foreign policy (Nye 2004).

4. **Social Balance**
   Societal cohesion depends on addressing inequalities and fostering inclusivity.

   - *Case Study*: Post-apartheid South Africa focused on balancing reconciliation with justice, contributing to nation-building (Gibson 2004).

Application of the Law

- **Policy Design:** Balanced policies consider short-term needs and long-term impacts, ensuring sustainable progress.
- **Crisis Management:** Nations that balance preparation with adaptability are better equipped to handle economic recessions, pandemics, or natural disasters.
- **Geopolitical Strategy:** Balancing relationships with rival powers prevents alliances from becoming overly dependent or adversarial.
  - *Example*: India's balancing act between the U.S. and Russia in its foreign policy demonstrates strategic equilibrium (Tellis 2019).

Lessons Learned

1. **Avoid Extremes:** Nations that lean too heavily into one domain, such as military expansion at the expense of social development, risk long-term instability.
2. **Foster Resilience:** Balance creates systems that can absorb shocks and adapt to crises without collapsing.
3. **Integrate Diverse Perspectives:** A balanced approach requires input from multiple sectors, ensuring holistic and comprehensive decisions.
4. **Prioritize Flexibility:** The ability to recalibrate balances based on changing circumstances is essential for sustained success.

Conclusion

The Law of Balance is a critical framework for achieving stability and success in geopolitics. Nations that understand and apply this principle across political, economic, military, and social dimensions can navigate complexities, sustain power, and foster global leadership. Policymakers must actively evaluate and adjust balances to address both immediate challenges and long-term goals.

References

1. Gibson, James L. *Overcoming Apartheid: Can Truth Reconcile a Divided Nation?* New York: Russell Sage Foundation, 2004. Available at: https://www.russellsage.org/publications/overcoming-apartheid.

2. Linder, Wolf. *Swiss Democracy: Possible Solutions to Conflict in Multicultural Societies.* 3rd ed. New York: Palgrave Macmillan, 2010. Available at: https://www.palgrave.com/gp/book/9780230232049.

3. Nye, Joseph S. *Soft Power: The Means to Success in World Politics.* New York: PublicAffairs, 2004. Available at: https://www.publicaffairsbooks.com/titles/joseph-nye/soft-power/9781586483067/.

4. Streeck, Wolfgang. "German Capitalism: Does It Exist? Can It Survive?" *New Political Economy* 2, no. 2 (1997): 237–256. Available at: https://doi.org/10.1080/13563469708406290.

5. Tellis, Ashley J. "India's Balancing Act in Foreign Policy." *Carnegie Endowment for International Peace,* 2019. Available at: https://carnegieendowment.org/2019/05/20/india-s-balancing-act-in-foreign-policy-pub-79256.

SECTION 16: THE LAW OF ASYMMETRY

Abstract

The Law of Asymmetry highlights the ability of weaker nations or groups to counterbalance more powerful adversaries by leveraging unconventional tactics, emerging technologies, or innovative strategies. This principle has been central to historical and modern conflicts, allowing less-resource entities to achieve disproportionate outcomes.

Introduction

Asymmetry in geopolitics refers to exploiting disparities in power, resources, or capabilities to neutralize more vigorous opponents. From guerrilla warfare to cyberattacks, asymmetric strategies redefine the rules of engagement.

Key Components of The Law of Asymmetry

1. **Unconventional Warfare**
   Asymmetric tactics often use non-traditional approaches, such as guerrilla warfare or terrorism, to counter superior military forces.
   - *Case Study*: The Vietnam War demonstrated how guerrilla warfare tactics allowed the Viet Cong to resist U.S. military power (Krepinevich 1986).
2. **Technological Leverage**
   Emerging technologies can offset conventional disadvantages by providing innovative tools for disruption.
   - *Modern Example*: The use of drones and cyberattacks by non-state actors like ISIS illustrates technological asymmetry (Klausen 2015).
3. **Economic and Diplomatic Maneuvering**
   Weaker nations often employ economic and diplomatic strategies to pressure more powerful states.
   - *Case Study*: The European Union's sanctions on Russia following the annexation of Crimea limited Russia's economic maneuverability (Drezner 1999).

Application of the Law

- **Military Strategy:** Asymmetric warfare remains critical for smaller powers to challenge dominant adversaries.
    - *Example:* Ukraine's resistance to Russian aggression has been bolstered by asymmetric tactics, including drones and guerrilla-style counterattacks (Kofman 2022).
- **Cyber Strategy:** Cyberattacks provide low-cost, high-impact options for disrupting adversaries' critical infrastructure.
    - *Case Study:* North Korea's 2014 Sony hack demonstrates how smaller nations can use cyber capabilities to exert global influence (Segal 2016).
- **Economic Strategy:** Targeted sanctions and economic restrictions are tools of asymmetric influence in geopolitics.
    - *Example:* The U.S.-China trade war reflects the asymmetric use of tariffs and supply chain manipulation to influence outcomes (Zhao 2020).

Lessons Learned

1. **Adaptability is Key:** Asymmetric strategies succeed by exploiting vulnerabilities and adapting to changing conditions.
2. **Innovation Over Resources:** Creativity and innovation often outweigh raw power in geopolitical contests.
3. **Mitigate Overreliance:** While effective, asymmetric strategies must be balanced with broader goals to avoid overreliance and escalation.
4. **Focus on Long-Term Gains:** Asymmetric tactics can achieve short-term victories but must align with sustainable strategic objectives.

Conclusion

The Law of Asymmetry demonstrates that weaker actors can effectively challenge dominant powers through innovation, adaptability, and unconventional tactics. By understanding and applying these strategies, nations, and organizations can navigate power imbalances and achieve significant geopolitical outcomes.

References

1. Krepinevich, Andrew F. *The Army and Vietnam*. Baltimore: Johns Hopkins University Press, 1986. Available at: https://jhupbooks.press.jhu.edu/title/army-and-vietnam.

2. Klausen, Jytte. "Tweeting the Jihad: Social Media Networks of Western Foreign Fighters in Syria and Iraq." *Studies in Conflict & Terrorism* 38, no. 1 (2015): 1–22. Available at: https://www.tandfonline.com/doi/full/10.1080/1057610X.2014.974948.

3. Drezner, Daniel W. *The Sanctions Paradox: Economic Statecraft and International Relations*. Cambridge: Cambridge University Press, 1999. Available at: https://doi.org/10.1017/CBO9780511612281.

4. Kofman, Michael. "Ukraine's Military Strategy Against Russia." *War on the Rocks*, February 2022. Available at: https://warontherocks.com/2022/02/ukraine-military-strategy.

5. Segal, Adam. *The Hacked World Order: How Nations Fight, Trade, Maneuver, and Manipulate in the Digital Age*. New York: Public Affairs, 2016. Available at: https://www.publicaffairsbooks.com/titles/adam-segal/the-hacked-world-order/9781610394161/.

6. Zhao, Suisheng. "The China-US Trade War and the Future of US-China Relations." *Asian Perspective* 44, no. 4 (2020): 635–648. Available at: https://doi.org/10.1353/apr.2020.0027.

SECTION 17: THE LAW OF STRATEGIC DEPTH

Abstract

The Law of Strategic Depth underscores the importance of geographic, economic, and logistical buffers that enhance a nation's ability to withstand adversities and project influence. Strategic depth can absorb shocks, delay enemy advances, and sustain prolonged engagements.

Introduction

Strategic depth refers to a nation's ability to leverage its geographic space, resource reserves, and infrastructure to ensure resilience against external threats. It has been a defining feature of military strategies and national security policies.

Key Components of The Law of Strategic Depth

1. **Geographic Depth**
   Nations with vast territories or defensible borders can better delay or repel adversaries.
   - *Historical Example*: Russia's vast geography provided strategic depth during Napoleon's invasion in 1812 and World War II, enabling a retreat and counteroffensive (Glantz 1995).
2. **Economic Resilience**
   Access to abundant resources and diversified economies allows nations to sustain prolonged engagements.
   - *Case Study*: During World War II, the United States' industrial base ensured a steady supply of arms and goods for the Allied forces (Kennedy 1987).
3. **Logistical Networks**
   Robust transportation and communication networks enhance the capacity to mobilize resources and respond to crises.
   - *Modern Example*: China's Belt and Road Initiative (BRI) expands its strategic depth by creating global economic and logistical ties (Rolland 2017).

Application of the Law

- **Military Strategy:** Nations with strategic depth can outlast more powerful adversaries by leveraging time and space.
  - *Example*: Afghanistan's rugged terrain and decentralized structure provided significant strategic depth during conflicts with the Soviet Union and the United States (Barfield 2010).
- **Economic Strategy:** Economic depth allows countries to withstand sanctions and economic downturns.
  - *Case Study*: Japan's post-World War II economic recovery leveraged strategic depth through industrial innovation and trade partnerships (Vogel 2006).
- **Global Influence:** Strategic depth enables nations to project power beyond their borders, influencing international trade and politics.
  - *Example*: The U.S. maintains strategic depth through military bases and alliances worldwide (Layne 2006).

Lessons Learned

1. **Invest in Infrastructure:** Building transportation, communication, and supply networks enhances strategic depth.
2. **Diversify Economic Resources:** A broad economic base increases resilience against external shocks.
3. **Leverage Alliances:** Partnerships extend strategic depth by pooling resources and capabilities.
4. **Adapt to Modern Challenges:** Strategic depth must evolve to address cyber threats and global supply chain dependencies.

Conclusion

The Law of Strategic Depth demonstrates that resilience and influence stem from the ability to absorb shocks and project power. By investing in geographic, economic, and logistical buffers, nations can enhance their capacity to manage crises and maintain stability. In an era of global interdependence, strategic depth remains a cornerstone of national security and international influence.

References

1. Barfield, Thomas. *Afghanistan: A Cultural and Political History*. Princeton, NJ: Princeton University Press, 2010. Available at: https://press.princeton.edu/books/paperback/9780691154411/afghanistan.

2. Glantz, David M. *When Titans Clashed: How the Red Army Stopped Hitler*. Lawrence, KS: University Press of Kansas, 1995. Available at: https://kansaspress.ku.edu/9780700607174/when-titans-clashed.

3. Kennedy, Paul. *The Rise and Fall of the Great Powers: Economic Change and Military Conflict from 1500 to 2000*. New York: Random House, 1987. Available at: https://www.penguinrandomhouse.com/books/324816/the-rise-and-fall-of-the-great-powers-by-paul-kennedy/.

4. Rolland, Nadège. *China's Eurasian Century? Political and Strategic Implications of the Belt and Road Initiative*. Seattle, WA: National Bureau of Asian Research, 2017. Available at: https://www.nbr.org/publication/chinas-eurasian-century-political-and-strategic-implications-of-the-belt-and-road-initiative/.

5. Vogel, Ezra F. *Japan as Number One: Lessons for America*. Cambridge, MA: Harvard University Press, 2006. Available at: https://www.hup.harvard.edu/catalog.php?isbn=9780674472074.

6. Layne, Christopher. *The Peace of Illusions: American Grand Strategy from 1940 to the Present*. Ithaca, NY: Cornell University Press, 2006. Available at: https://www.cornellpress.cornell.edu/book/9780801474110/the-peace-of-illusions/.

SECTION 18: THE LAW OF ENCIRCLEMENT

Abstract

The Law of Encirclement highlights the strategic importance of isolating adversaries through geographic, economic, and political means to weaken their influence and limit their options. This principle has been pivotal in military campaigns, economic sanctions, and alliance-building efforts.

Introduction

Encirclement is a fundamental strategy in geopolitics and military science. By surrounding an adversary with hostile forces, alliances, or economic barriers, nations can effectively neutralize threats and constrain enemy actions.

Key Components of The Law of Encirclement

1. **Geographic Encirclement**
   Physical encirclement surrounds an adversary's territory to cut off supply lines and strategic depth.
   - *Historical Example*: During World War II, the Allied Powers encircled Nazi Germany, leading to its eventual collapse (Beevor 2012).
2. **Economic Encirclement**
   Economic sanctions and trade barriers isolate nations from global markets, weakening their economies.
   - *Modern Example*: Sanctions imposed on Iran to curtail its nuclear ambitions exemplify economic encirclement (Drezner 1999).
3. **Political Encirclement**
   Diplomatic alliances can isolate an adversary by limiting their influence in international affairs.
   - *Case Study*: The Quad (U.S., Japan, India, Australia) serves as a counterbalance to China's growing influence in the Indo-Pacific (Green 2021).

Application of the Law

- **Military Strategy:** Geographic encirclement remains a vital tactic in warfare, as demonstrated during the Gulf War when coalition forces isolated Iraqi troops (Schwarzkopf 1992).
- **Economic Strategy:** Trade wars and economic sanctions create financial pressure, as seen in the U.S.-led sanctions on Russia following the annexation of Crimea (Mearsheimer 2014).
- **Diplomatic Strategy:** Political alliances like NATO enhance collective security and isolate adversaries through coordinated efforts (Kay 1998).

Lessons Learned

1. **Balance Aggression and Diplomacy:** While encirclement can weaken adversaries, it may provoke escalations if not managed carefully.
2. **Leverage Multilateral Approaches:** Encirclement strategies are most effective when implemented through alliances and coalitions.
3. **Adapt to Emerging Threats:** Modern encirclement strategies must incorporate cyber and informational dimensions.
4. **Avoid Overextension:** Overly aggressive encirclement can drain resources and destabilize alliances.

Conclusion

The Law of Encirclement remains a powerful strategy for neutralizing adversaries and shaping geopolitical outcomes. By employing geographic, economic, and political isolation, nations can constrain threats and assert dominance. However, successful implementation requires careful calibration to avoid unintended consequences and maintain global stability.

References

1. Beevor, Antony. *The Second World War.* London: Weidenfeld & Nicolson, 2012. Available at: https://www.weidenfeldandnicolson.co.uk/.

2. Drezner, Daniel W. *The Sanctions Paradox: Economic Statecraft and International Relations.* Cambridge: Cambridge University Press, 1999. Available at: https://doi.org/10.1017/CBO9780511612281.

3. Green, Michael. *By More Than Providence: Grand Strategy and American Power in the Asia Pacific Since 1783.* New York: Columbia University Press, 2021. Available at: https://cup.columbia.edu/.

4. Kay, Sean. *NATO and the Future of European Security.* Lanham, MD: Rowman & Littlefield, 1998. Available at: https://rowman.com/.

5. Mearsheimer, John J. "Why the Ukraine Crisis Is the West's Fault." *Foreign Affairs* 93, no. 5 (2014): 77–89. Available at: https://www.foreignaffairs.com/.

6. Schwarzkopf, H. Norman. *It Doesn't Take a Hero: The Autobiography of General H. Norman Schwarzkopf.* New York: Bantam Books, 1992. Available at: https://www.penguinrandomhouse.com/.

SECTION 19: THE LAW OF DETERRENCE

Abstract

The Law of Deterrence emphasizes the strategic use of threats, military capabilities, and alliances to prevent adversaries from taking undesirable actions. Deterrence has been central to global security since the Cold War, rooted in the principle of projecting credible consequences.

Introduction

Deterrence is a cornerstone of national security, designed to discourage adversaries by demonstrating the costs of aggression. While its classic applications stem from nuclear standoffs during the Cold War, deterrence strategies have diversified to include conventional forces, cyber capabilities, and economic measures.

Key Components of The Law of Deterrence

1. **Credibility**
   For deterrence to work, threats must be perceived as credible and enforceable.
   - *Example*: The U.S. extended deterrence through NATO during the Cold War, backed by its nuclear arsenal (Wohlstetter 1959).
2. **Proportionality**
   The response threatened must align with the scale of the potential aggression to avoid over-escalation.
   - *Modern Example*: The European Union's targeted sanctions on Russia after its annexation of Crimea deterred further territorial expansion while avoiding full-scale war (Drezner 1999).
3. **Capability Demonstration**
   Regular demonstrations of military or economic strength reinforce the effectiveness of deterrence.
   - *Case Study*: North Korea's missile tests aim to deter U.S. military actions by showcasing its growing capabilities (Sagan 1996).

Application of the Law

- **Military Strategy:** Deterrence through a robust military presence has been key to maintaining peace in the Korean Peninsula.
    - *Example:* The U.S. maintains military bases in South Korea and Japan as a deterrent against North Korean aggression (Cha 2018).
- **Cyber Strategy:** Nations leverage cyber capabilities as a deterrent and retaliatory measure.
    - *Case Study:* The U.S. Cyber Command's "defend forward" strategy aims to deter cyberattacks by preemptively targeting adversaries' networks (Nakasone 2020).
- **Economic Strategy:** Economic sanctions serve as tools of deterrence to influence state behavior.
    - *Example:* Sanctions on Iran were designed to deter nuclear development, restricting its access to global financial systems (Maloney 2021).

Lessons Learned

1. **Maintain Credibility:** A deterrent that lacks credibility risks emboldening adversaries rather than deterring them.
2. **Avoid Overreach:** Proportional deterrence is crucial to maintaining stability and avoiding unnecessary escalation.
3. **Adapt to New Domains:** Deterrence strategies must evolve to address cyber threats, space militarization, and economic dependencies.
4. **Strengthen Alliances:** Collective deterrence through alliances enhances the credibility and reach of deterrent measures.

Conclusion

The Law of Deterrence remains a vital strategy for preventing aggression and maintaining global stability. By aligning credibility, proportionality, and demonstrable capabilities, nations can deter adversaries effectively. However, the evolving nature of threats necessitates continuous adaptation of deterrence strategies to ensure their relevance and effectiveness.

References

1. Cha, Victor D. *The Impossible State: North Korea, Past and Future.* New York: HarperCollins, 2018. Available at: https://www.harpercollins.com/.

2. Drezner, Daniel W. *The Sanctions Paradox: Economic Statecraft and International Relations.* Cambridge: Cambridge University Press, 1999. Available at: https://doi.org/10.1017/CBO9780511612281.

3. Maloney, Suzanne. *Iran's Political Economy since the Revolution.* Cambridge: Cambridge University Press, 2021. Available at: https://www.cambridge.org/core/books/irans-political-economy-since-the-revolution/.

4. Nakasone, Paul. "A Cyber Force for Persistent Operations." *Joint Force Quarterly* 92 (2020): 10–16. Available at: https://ndupress.ndu.edu/.

5. Sagan, Scott D. "Why Do States Build Nuclear Weapons?: Three Models in Search of a Bomb." *International Security* 21, no. 3 (1996): 54–86. Available at: https://doi.org/10.2307/2539273.

6. Wohlstetter, Albert. "The Delicate Balance of Terror." *Foreign Affairs* 37, no. 2 (1959): 211–234. Available at: https://www.foreignaffairs.com/.

SECTION 20: THE LAW OF PROXIMITY

Abstractt
The Law of Proximity emphasizes the strategic importance of geographic and relational closeness in geopolitics. Nations prioritize their immediate neighbors and regional spheres of influence due to shared borders, economic interdependence, and potential conflict or cooperation.

Introduction

Proximity in geopolitics refers to the influence exerted by nations based on their geographic closeness. It is critical in determining a state's priorities, alliances, and potential threats. Proximity often dictates the allocation of resources, the intensity of diplomatic efforts, and the urgency of conflict resolution.

Key Components of The Law of Proximity

1. **Geopolitical Influence**
   Nations naturally focus on nearby regions, viewing them as extensions of their security perimeter.
   - *Historical Example*: The Monroe Doctrine exemplifies the U.S.'s focus on the Western Hemisphere as a zone of strategic interest (Perkins 1963).
2. **Economic Interdependence**
   Neighboring states are often key trade partners due to geographic closeness and shared infrastructure.
   - *Case Study*: The European Union relies on regional proximity to foster economic integration and stability (Moravcsik 1998).
3. **Conflict and Cooperation**
   Geographic proximity increases the likelihood of both conflict and collaboration.
   - *Modern Example*: India and Pakistan's proximity has fueled decades of conflict and necessitated diplomatic engagement (Ganguly 1994).

Application of the Law

- **Security Strategy:** Nations prioritize securing borders and establishing control over their immediate vicinity.
    - *Example*: Russia's actions in Ukraine reflect its perception of NATO expansion as threatening its proximal sphere of influence (Mearsheimer 2014).
- **Economic Strategy:** Regional trade agreements enhance financial stability and growth among neighboring states.
    - *Case Study*: The North American Free Trade Agreement (NAFTA) significantly increased trade among the U.S., Canada, and Mexico by capitalizing on geographic proximity (Hufbauer 1993).
- **Diplomatic Strategy:** Proximity fosters collaboration through shared institutions and regional initiatives.
    - *Example*: The Association of Southeast Asian Nations (ASEAN) leverages proximity to address regional issues collectively (Acharya 2017).

Lessons Learned

1. **Address Neighborly Relations:** Stable relations with neighbors are a cornerstone of long-term security and prosperity.
2. **Leverage Regional Opportunities:** Geographic proximity can be a foundation for regional economic and security cooperation.
3. **Balance Proximal Threats:** Nations must find an equilibrium between securing borders and avoiding unnecessary provocation.
4. **Adapt to Shifting Proximity Dynamics:** Technological advancements, such as cyber capabilities, have redefined the concept of proximity in modern geopolitics.

Conclusion

The Law of Proximity underscores the importance of geographic closeness in shaping national priorities and strategies. While proximity offers opportunities for economic and security cooperation, it also heightens the risk of conflict. Policymakers must navigate these dynamics carefully, leveraging geographic proximity to strengthen regional stability while addressing potential threats.

References

1. Acharya, Amitav. *The Making of Southeast Asia: International Relations of a Region.* Ithaca, NY: Cornell University Press, 2017. Available at: https://www.cornellpress.cornell.edu/.

2. Ganguly, Sumit. *The Origins of War in South Asia: Indo-Pakistani Conflicts since 1947.* Boulder, CO: Westview Press, 1994. Available at: https://www.routledge.com/.

3. Hufbauer, Gary Clyde. *NAFTA Revisited: Achievements and Challenges.* Washington, DC: Peterson Institute for International Economics, 1993. Available at: https://www.piie.com/.

4. Mearsheimer, John J. "Why the Ukraine Crisis Is the West's Fault." *Foreign Affairs* 93, no. 5 (2014): 77–89. Available at: https://www.foreignaffairs.com/.

5. Moravcsik, Andrew. "Preferences and Power in the European Community: A Liberal Intergovernmentalist Approach." *Journal of Common Market Studies* 31, no. 4 (1998): 473–524. Available at: https://doi.org/10.1111/jcms.1998.31.issue-4.

6. Perkins, Bradford. *The Creation of a Republican Empire, 1776-1865.* Cambridge: Cambridge University Press, 1963. Available at: https://www.cambridge.org/core/books/creation-of-a-republican-empire-17761865.

SECTION 21: THE LAW OF RELEVANCE

Abstract

The Law of Relevance emphasizes aligning national strategies with current global and regional dynamics. Nations that maintain relevance through adaptive policies, innovative technologies, and strategic alliances can better secure their interests and influence.

Introduction

Relevance in geopolitics is defined by a nation's ability to remain integral to the global order, regional stability, and the international economy. Achieving relevance requires continuous adaptation to shifting power dynamics, technological advancements, and emerging challenges.

Key Components of The Law of Relevance

1. **Technological Innovation**
   Nations that lead in technological advancements gain significant geopolitical relevance.

   - *Example*: The U.S.'s dominance in technological innovation during the 20th century established it as a global leader in economic and military power (Freeman 2002).

2. **Economic Integration**
   A nation's integration into global markets enhances its relevance in international relations.

   - *Case Study*: China's Belt and Road Initiative (BRI) has increased its economic relevance across Asia, Africa, and Europe (Rolland 2017).

3. **Diplomatic Flexibility**
   Adapting to evolving global alliances and conflicts ensures long-term relevance.

   - *Modern Example*: Turkey's balancing act between NATO and Russia demonstrates the importance of diplomatic flexibility in maintaining geopolitical relevance (Altunışık 2021).

Application of the Law

- **Military Strategy:** Maintaining cutting-edge military capabilities ensures relevance in security alliances and deterrence efforts.
    - *For example,* Israel's advanced defense technologies, such as the Iron Dome, bolster its regional relevance (Katz and Bohbot 2017).
- **Economic Strategy:** Building trade networks and engaging in multilateral agreements enhance relevance in the global economy.
    - *Case Study*: The European Union's influence is rooted in its integrated economic model and trade partnerships (Moravcsik 1998).
- **Global Leadership:** Nations that address global challenges, such as climate change or pandemics, secure their relevance in international forums.
    - *Example*: Germany's leadership in renewable energy policy has reinforced its role as a key player in the European Union and beyond (Meckling 2011).

Lessons Learned

1. **Invest in Innovation:** Technological and economic innovation are critical for sustaining relevance in an evolving global order.
2. **Maintain Diplomatic Agility:** Adapting alliances and relationships ensures flexibility in addressing geopolitical shifts.
3. **Engage in Global Challenges:** Tackling issues like climate change, public health, and cyber threats enhances a nation's global standing.
4. **Focus on Sustainability:** Relevance must be maintained with sustainable policies that balance short-term gains and long-term interests.

Conclusion

The Law of Relevance highlights the importance of staying integral to global systems and regional stability. Nations that adapt to changing circumstances through innovation, diplomacy, and leadership secure their influence and resilience. Policymakers must prioritize relevance to navigate the complexities of a rapidly changing geopolitical landscape.

References

1. Altunışık, Meliha B. "Turkey Between NATO and Russia: Geopolitical Balancing in the 21st Century." *Turkish Studies* 22, no. 3 (2021): 289–307. Available at: https://doi.org/10.1080/14683849.2020.1821074.

2. Freeman, Chris. *The Economics of Industrial Innovation.* Cambridge: MIT Press, 2002. Available at: https://mitpress.mit.edu/books/economics-industrial-innovation.

3. Katz, Yaakov, and Amir Bohbot. *The Weapon Wizards: How Israel Became a High-Tech Military Superpower.* New York: St. Martin's Press, 2017. Available at: https://us.macmillan.com/books/9781250118744/theweaponwizards.

4. Meckling, Jonas. *Carbon Coalitions: Business, Climate Politics, and the Rise of Emissions Trading.* Cambridge: MIT Press, 2011. Available at: https://mitpress.mit.edu/books/carbon-coalitions.

5. Moravcsik, Andrew. "Preferences and Power in the European Community: A Liberal Intergovernmentalist Approach." *Journal of Common Market Studies* 31, no. 4 (1998): 473–524. Available at: https://doi.org/10.1111/jcms.1998.31.issue-4.

6. Rolland, Nadège. *China's Eurasian Century? Political and Strategic Implications of the Belt and Road Initiative.* Seattle, WA: National Bureau of Asian Research, 2017. Available at: https://www.nbr.org/publication/chinas-eurasian-century-political-and-strategic-implications-of-the-belt-and-road-initiative/.

SECTION 23: THE LAW OF RESILIENCE

Abstract
The Law of Resilience highlights the importance of adaptability and endurance in facing challenges. Nations that prioritize resilience through strong institutions, diversified economies, and robust security frameworks can recover from crises and maintain stability.

Introduction

Resilience in geopolitics refers to a nation's ability to withstand and recover from external and internal disruptions, including wars, economic shocks, and natural disasters. It measures survival, adaptability, and growth in the face of adversity.

Key Components of The Law of Resilience

1. **Institutional Strength**
   Resilient nations rely on strong, adaptable institutions that maintain stability during crises.

   - *Example*: The United States federal system allowed decentralized responses during the COVID-19 pandemic, showcasing institutional adaptability (Kettl 2020).

2. **Economic Diversification**
   Diversified economies can better absorb shocks and recover from disruptions.

   - *Case Study*: Norway's sovereign wealth fund, built on oil revenues, has provided economic resilience during global downturns (Holden 2013).

3. **Social Cohesion**
   A united population contributes to resilience by fostering trust and collective action.

   - *Example*: Japan's societal response to the 2011 Fukushima disaster reflected strong social cohesion and collective resilience (Kingston 2012).

4. **Robust Security Frameworks**
   Nations with comprehensive defense and intelligence systems are better equipped to handle threats.

- *Modern Example*: Israel's Iron Dome system exemplifies resilience in responding to external missile threats (Katz and Bohbot 2017).

Application of the Law

- **Policy Design**: Resilient policies focus on long-term sustainability and adaptability.
  - *Example*: Germany's energy transition strategy (Energiewende) illustrates a proactive approach to building resilience in energy supply and climate policy (Meckling 2011).
- **Economic Strategy**: Investing in diversification and risk mitigation enhances economic resilience.
  - *Case Study*: Singapore's emphasis on innovation and diversification has made it one of the most resilient economies globally (Low 2012).
- **Security Strategy**: Comprehensive security frameworks, including cyber defenses, bolster resilience against emerging threats.
  - *Example*: Estonia's development of robust cyber resilience following the 2007 cyberattacks demonstrates the importance of proactive measures (Tikk 2011).

Lessons Learned

1. **Invest in Institutions**: Resilient governance systems can better respond to crises and sustain stability.
2. **Foster Social Unity**: A cohesive society enhances resilience through collective action and mutual trust.
3. **Prioritize Diversification**: Economic and resource diversification reduces vulnerability to specific shocks.
4. **Plan for Long-Term Resilience**: Strategic energy, technology, and infrastructure investments ensure sustainable growth.

Conclusion

The Law of Resilience emphasizes the importance of adaptability, unity, and preparedness in maintaining national power and stability. Nations that invest in resilience across institutional, economic, and social dimensions can recover from crises and emerge stronger. Policymakers must prioritize resilience to navigate the complexities of the modern geopolitical landscape.

References

1. Holden, Steinar. *Avoiding the Oil Curse: The Case of Norway.* Oxford: Oxford University Press, 2013. Available at: https://global.oup.com/.

2. Katz, Yaakov, and Amir Bohbot. *The Weapon Wizards: How Israel Became a High-Tech Military Superpower.* New York: St. Martin's Press, 2017. Available at: https://us.macmillan.com/books/9781250118744/theweaponwizards.

3. Kingston, Jeff. *Contemporary Japan: History, Politics, and Social Change since the 1980s.* New York: Wiley, 2012. Available at: https://www.wiley.com/en-us/Contemporary+Japan.

4. Kettl, Donald F. *The Divided States of America: Why Federalism Doesn't Work.* Princeton, NJ: Princeton University Press, 2020. Available at: https://press.princeton.edu/books/hardcover/9780691204345/the-divided-states-of-america.

5. Low, Linda. *Singapore: From Third World to First.* Singapore: World Scientific Publishing, 2012. Available at: https://www.worldscientific.com/.

6. Meckling, Jonas. *Carbon Coalitions: Business, Climate Politics, and the Rise of Emissions Trading.* Cambridge: MIT Press, 2011. Available at: https://mitpress.mit.edu/books/carbon-coalitions.

7. Tikk, Eneken. "Cyber Attacks Against Estonia: Legal Lessons Learned." *Tallinn Manual on the International Law Applicable to Cyber Warfare,* NATO CCD COE, 2011. Available at: https://ccdcoe.org/.

SECTION 23: THE LAW OF INNOVATION

Abstract

The Law of Innovation emphasizes the pivotal role of creativity and technological advancement in maintaining geopolitical relevance and addressing emerging challenges. Nations that foster innovation gain competitive economic, military, and diplomatic advantages.

Introduction

Innovation in geopolitics refers to developing new technologies, strategies, and ideas to address evolving challenges and capitalize on opportunities. From military advancements to economic reforms, innovation has been a driving force behind the success and resilience of nations.

Key Components of The Law of Innovation

1. **Technological Advancement**
   Nations that invest in research and development gain significant military and economic power advantages.

   - *Example*: The Manhattan Project during World War II revolutionized warfare and established the U.S. as a global superpower (Rhodes 1986).

2. **Economic Modernization**
   Innovative economic policies and practices enable nations to adapt to global market changes.

   - *Case Study*: China's economic transformation through reforms and technological advancements has reshaped global trade dynamics (Zeng 2009).

3. **Strategic Adaptation**
   Strategy innovation allows nations to respond effectively to unconventional threats.

   - *Modern Example*: Israel's adaptation to asymmetric warfare through advanced defense systems like the Iron Dome demonstrates strategic innovation (Katz and Bohbot 2017).

Application of the Law

- **Military Strategy**: Developing cutting-edge technologies and tactics ensures superiority and deterrence.
    - *Example*: The U.S. Pentagon's investment in artificial intelligence and robotics highlights the integration of innovation in military strategy (Kania 2018).
- **Economic Strategy**: Diversifying and modernizing industries fosters global competitiveness.
    - *Case Study*: Germany's Industry 4.0 initiative showcases innovation in manufacturing and technology-driven growth (Drath 2011).
- **Diplomatic Strategy**: Innovative diplomacy and international collaboration approaches can resolve complex global challenges.
    - *Example*: The Paris Climate Agreement demonstrates innovative frameworks for global consensus on climate action (Hale 2016).

Lessons Learned

1. **Invest in Research and Development**: Sustained investment in R&D drives technological and economic innovation.
2. **Encourage Public-Private Partnerships**: Collaboration between government and industry accelerates innovation.
3. **Adapt to Emerging Threats**: Innovation must address unconventional and transnational threats like cyber warfare and climate change.
4. **Promote Inclusive Policies**: Broad-based innovation policies that include diverse stakeholders yield more sustainable outcomes.

Conclusion

The Law of Innovation underscores the importance of creativity, adaptability, and technological advancement in geopolitics. Nations that prioritize innovation across military, economic, and diplomatic domains can secure competitive advantages and effectively navigate complex global challenges. Policymakers must foster environments that encourage innovation to maintain strategic relevance and leadership.

References

1. Drath, Rainer. "Industry 4.0: Intelligent Manufacturing in the Fourth Industrial Revolution." *Automation in Manufacturing*, 2011. Available at: https://www.automationworld.com/.

2. Hale, Thomas. "The Paris Climate Agreement: The Start of a New Era in International Climate Diplomacy." *International Affairs* 92, no. 5 (2016): 1107–1125. Available at: https://academic.oup.com/ia/article/92/5/1107/2688531.

3. Kania, Elsa B. "Artificial Intelligence and China's Military Innovation." *Strategic Studies Quarterly* 12, no. 2 (2018): 24–45. Available at: https://www.airuniversity.af.edu/.

4. Katz, Yaakov, and Amir Bohbot. *The Weapon Wizards: How Israel Became a High-Tech Military Superpower*. New York: St. Martin's Press, 2017. Available at: https://us.macmillan.com/books/9781250118744/theweaponwizards.

5. Rhodes, Richard. *The Making of the Atomic Bomb*. New York: Simon & Schuster, 1986. Available at: https://www.simonandschuster.com/.

6. Zeng, Douglas Zhihua. *Building Engines for Growth and Competitiveness in China: Experience with Special Economic Zones and Industrial Clusters*. Washington, DC: World Bank Publications, 2009. Available at: https://openknowledge.worldbank.org/.

SECTION 24: THE LAW OF CONTINUITY

Abstract

The Law of Continuity emphasizes maintaining consistent policies, strategies, and alliances to ensure long-term stability and influence. Continuity allows nations to build trust, sustain progress, and effectively respond to changing circumstances without losing sight of overarching goals.

Introduction

Continuity in geopolitics involves consistently applying strategic principles and policies over time. While adaptability is crucial, frequent changes in direction can undermine trust, disrupt progress, and weaken alliances.

Key Components of The Law of Continuity

1. **Policy Stability**
   Stable policies foster trust and predictability among allies and within domestic constituencies.
   - *Example*: The United States' containment strategy during the Cold War reflected decades of consistent foreign policy (Gaddis 2005).
2. **Institutional Strength**
   Robust institutions ensure continuity in governance and strategy, even during leadership transitions.
   - *Case Study*: The British parliamentary system exemplifies institutional continuity, contributing to its global influence across centuries (Bogdanor 1996).
3. **Strategic Partnerships**
   Continuity in alliances reinforces trust and enhances long-term collaboration.
   - *Modern Example*: The North Atlantic Treaty Organization (NATO) has maintained consistent principles of collective defense since its founding in 1949 (Kay 1998).

Application of the Law

- **Military Strategy:** Continuity in defense policies ensures readiness and deters adversaries.
    - *For example,* Israel's long-term commitment to military preparedness has sustained its security in a volatile region (Katz and Bohbot 2017).
- **Economic Strategy:** Consistent economic policies foster investor confidence and international trade relations.
    - *Case Study:* Germany's adherence to fiscal discipline and export-driven growth reflects the benefits of economic continuity (Streeck 2011).
- **Diplomatic Strategy:** Long-term diplomatic engagements, such as peace processes, require continuity to achieve lasting results.
    - *Example:* The European Union's decades-long integration efforts demonstrate the power of sustained collaboration (Moravcsik 1998).

Lessons Learned

1. **Foster Policy Consistency:** Stable and predictable policies build trust and credibility with allies and citizens.
2. **Invest in Institutions:** Strong institutions provide a foundation for continuity, ensuring stability during transitions.
3. **Balance Continuity with Adaptability:** Continuity should be flexible enough to incorporate necessary changes while preserving core principles.
4. **Prioritize Long-Term Goals:** Short-term gains should not compromise pursuing enduring objectives.

Conclusion

The Law of Continuity underscores the importance of steady, consistent strategies in maintaining geopolitical influence and stability. While flexibility is necessary, continuity in policies, alliances, and institutions provides a foundation for sustained progress and trust. Policymakers must strike a balance between continuity and adaptability to navigate the complexities of global politics effectively.

References

1. Bogdanor, Vernon. *The Monarchy and the Constitution.* Oxford: Oxford University Press, 1996. Available at: https://www.oup.com/.

2. Gaddis, John Lewis. *Strategies of Containment: A Critical Appraisal of American National Security Policy During the Cold War.* New York: Oxford University Press, 2005. Available at: https://global.oup.com/.

3. Katz, Yaakov, and Amir Bohbot. *The Weapon Wizards: How Israel Became a High-Tech Military Superpower.* New York: St. Martin's Press, 2017. Available at: https://us.macmillan.com/books/9781250118744/theweaponwizards.

4. Kay, Sean. *NATO and the Future of European Security.* Lanham, MD: Rowman & Littlefield, 1998. Available at: https://rowman.com/.

5. Moravcsik, Andrew. "Preferences and Power in the European Community: A Liberal Intergovernmentalist Approach." *Journal of Common Market Studies* 31, no. 4 (1998): 473–524. Available at: https://doi.org/10.1111/jcms.1998.31.issue-4.

6. Streeck, Wolfgang. "The Crises of Democratic Capitalism." *New Left Review* 71 (2011): 5–29. Available at: https://newleftreview.org/.

SECTION 25: THE LAW OF STRATEGIC PATIENCE

Abstract
The Law of Strategic Patience emphasizes the importance of long-term vision and calculated decision-making in geopolitics. Nations that exercise patience can avoid rash actions, leverage timing to their advantage, and achieve sustainable outcomes.

Introduction

Strategic patience is the deliberate practice of withholding immediate action in favor of long-term goals. This principle requires foresight, discipline, and the ability to tolerate short-term uncertainties for greater strategic benefits. In geopolitics, patience has often been the key to resolving conflicts, strengthening alliances, and achieving lasting influence.

Key Components of The Law of Strategic Patience

1. **Long-Term Vision**
   Strategic patience is anchored in clear, long-term objectives that guide decision-making.

   - *Example*: The United States' policy of containment during the Cold War demonstrated patience by avoiding direct conflict while gradually weakening the Soviet Union (Gaddis 2005).

2. **Calculated Timing**
   Timing plays a crucial role in maximizing the impact of actions and decisions.

   - *Case Study*: China's gradual economic reforms, beginning in the late 20th century, illustrate the importance of strategic timing in achieving global economic dominance (Zeng 2009).

3. **Resilience in Uncertainty**
   Patience involves enduring uncertainty and resisting pressure for immediate results.

   - *Modern Example*: The European Union's prolonged negotiations with the United Kingdom over Brexit showcased strategic patience in securing favorable terms (Menon and Fowler, 2020).

Application of the Law

- **Military Strategy:** Patience in military engagements prevents escalation and ensures sustainable victories.
    - *Example*: The U.S.'s surge strategy in Iraq (2007) was implemented after years of assessing the conflict, showcasing calculated military patience (Petraeus 2008).
- **Economic Strategy:** Long-term investments and gradual reforms yield sustained economic growth.
    - *Case Study*: Singapore's patient development of its economy through targeted investments in education and infrastructure reflects this principle (Low 2012).
- **Diplomatic Strategy:** Prolonged negotiations often yield more durable agreements and alliances.
    - *Example*: The 2015 Iran Nuclear Deal (JCPOA) was achieved after years of strategic patience and multilateral diplomacy (Maloney 2021).

Lessons Learned

1. **Define Clear Objectives:** Strategic patience requires a clear understanding of long-term goals.
2. **Balance Patience and Action:** While patience is vital, excessive delays can create missed opportunities.
3. **Resist Impulsive Decisions:** Patience demands resisting the temptation of short-term gains that undermine broader objectives.
4. **Build Resilient Systems:** Robust institutions and alliances support the endurance required for strategic patience.

Conclusion

The Law of Strategic Patience underscores the value of long-term vision and calculated restraint in achieving geopolitical success. Nations with patience can navigate complexities, mitigate risks, and secure enduring outcomes. Policymakers must foster discipline, resilience, and strategic foresight to leverage the full potential of patience in global strategy.

References

1. Gaddis, John Lewis. *Strategies of Containment: A Critical Appraisal of American National Security Policy During the Cold War.* New York: Oxford University Press, 2005. Available at: https://global.oup.com/.

2. Low, Linda. *Singapore: From Third World to First.* Singapore: World Scientific Publishing, 2012. Available at: https://www.worldscientific.com/.

3. Maloney, Suzanne. *Iran's Political Economy since the Revolution.* Cambridge: Cambridge University Press, 2021. Available at: https://www.cambridge.org/core/books/irans-political-economy-since-the-revolution/.

4. Menon, Anand, and Geoffrey Fowler. *Brexit and Beyond: Rethinking the Futures of Europe.* London: UCL Press, 2020. Available at: https://www.uclpress.co.uk/.

5. Petraeus, David H. "The Surge in Iraq: One Year Later." *Military Review* 88, no. 1 (2008): 2–15. Available at: https://www.armyupress.army.mil/.

6. Zeng, Douglas Zhihua. *Building Engines for Growth and Competitiveness in China: Experience with Special Economic Zones and Industrial Clusters.* Washington, DC: World Bank Publications, 2009. Available at: https://openknowledge.worldbank.org/.

www.ingramcontent.com/pod-product-compliance
Lightning Source LLC
LaVergne TN
LVHW082356200926
848481LV00012B/3583